DAD
RULES

Also by Michael Milligan:

Grandma Rules (with Jill Milligan)

Grandpa Rules

Mom Rules (with Jill Milligan)

DAD RULES

Notes on Fatherhood, the World's Best Job

Michael Milligan and Tom Lynch

Illustrations by
Adam Wallenta

Skyhorse Publishing

Skyhorse Publishing books may be purchased in bulk at special discounts for sales promotion, corporate gifts, fund raising, or educational purposes. Special editions can also be created to specifications. For details, contact Special Sales Department, 307 West 36th Street, Floor 11, Suite 903, New York, NY 10018 or info@skyhorsepublishing.com.

www.skyhorsepublishing.com

10 9 8 7 6 5 4 3 2 1

Library of Congress Cataloging-in-Publication data is available on file.

ISBN: 978-1-62873-769-1

Cover design by Danielle Ceccolini

Printed in China

This book is for Bernie Milligan,
who exposed his son to writing and to laughter.
And to the entire Lynch brigade.

CONTENTS

PREFACE

Whether your kids call you "Dad," "Pop," or "Daddy,"—and whether your loving spouse refers to you as "Honey," "Sweetie," or "Oh, crap, what did you do now?"—*Dad Rules* is an extremely important training text for dads of all experience levels: longtime dads, new dads, and dads-to-be.

OK, so "extremely" is a bit much . . . and maybe "important" is, too. But we do know that *Dad Rules* will put a smile on the face of any man who has navigated—or is about to navigate—the often curvy, pothole-filled roads of fatherhood. And the responsibility of being behind the wheel on such an unpredictable journey can often be unsettling, especially with a two-year-old in the backseat, happily smearing his ice cream over every inch of available window, and your wife next to you, offering her always helpful advice to "Slow down," "Turn left at the next . . . aw, you missed it," and "I knew we should have brought a map."

But fear not, men, because now you have *Dad Rules* to act as your GPS! First, we'll guide you from that life-altering moment when your wife says, "Honey, we need to talk," but you misunderstand and wonder how in the world she found out about the $1,200 you laid out for new golf clubs. Then we'll take you through pregnancy and birthing classes (even offering a few excuses for missing a session or two), followed by an entirely plausible story you can tell the emergency room physician to explain how your brand new nine iron found itself lodged in your backside.

The next stop will be the birth center, where we will lead you through the birthing process and try to get you acclimated to just a few of the unflattering names your wife will undoubtedly call you, particularly during the final moments immediately before your precious little one makes an entrance.

But as soon as that beautiful, spectacular little person you helped create peers at you with those dark brown eyes, all of that is forgotten; and as you hold your one-minute-old infant for the very first time, you experience a feeling you've never felt before . . . in fact, it's one you never even imagined.

Congratulations, Dad. And as you take in a deep breath of that unmistakable new baby smell, you vow that you will love this child forever.

And you will. But it will not always be as easy as it is at that moment, because all a newborn does for the first month or so is take food in, then pass it back out; a feat performed with amazing regularity. And how will all this change your life? Well, only two or three years ago, your favorite sentence was, "Who's in for beer pong?" Now it's, "Hey, look everybody, my little cutie made poo-poo again!"

Then, before you know it, your little genius will begin making sounds, which will eventually become words, which will eventually become sentences.

Life sentences.

Sentences like, "Why? Because I don't want to!" will progress to, "The problem with my grades is that my teacher hates me." Next, you'll be hearing things like, "Chill, Dad. It's not like we don't have car insurance," and then, the most dreaded words of all, which dads often hear after a child graduates from college: "Aaaahhh, it sure is nice to be back in my old room again."

So fasten your seat belt, keep your eyes on the road, and enjoy the journey of being a dad. It will be quite a trip.

DAD
RULES

ONE

GAME ON!

It's a beautiful Saturday afternoon. The sun is shining; the birds are chirping; and you? You feel like you might vomit. That's because you are on your company's softball team; it's the bottom of the last inning of your first game of the year, the bases are loaded, and you are at bat. What's more, there are two outs and your team trails by one run. It all comes down to you. But what's really got your stomach tumbling is something that you never shared with your teammates: you suck at softball. In high school, you concentrated on more cerebral pursuits. You lettered in diving and served as president of the Computer Club (two terms!).

But of course you didn't mention any of this when your boss was scrambling for enough players to field a team. In fact, you told him you were quite a baseball player back in the day. If it weren't for the arm injury, who knows how far you could have gone? You did this for two reasons: One, you are a guy; embellishing your past athletic prowess is in your DNA, just like scratching yourself and forgetting to zip your pants. Two, as one of the company's newest hires, you figured being on a company team would provide an excellent opportunity to meet people in other departments, to enjoy the camaraderie of being part of a group, and to get some exercise. "To totally humiliate yourself" was not on your list.

The umpire calls "Strike one!" for everyone to hear. You look over to the bench. Your coach, who is also your boss, wears an incredulous expression that says, "This guy played baseball in high school? At where? Saint Dweeb's?"

You stare out at the pitcher as you recall your previous two at-bats.

Your first time up, you struck out; but your coach/boss said it was a horrible call, so you felt somewhat exonerated. The second time, you swung mightily and dinked one all the way back to the pitcher, who threw you out at first by about twenty-five feet.

As you dig in for the next pitch, you hear their third baseman yell to the pitcher, "C'mon, Jenny, just put it over. This guy can't hit!"

"Oh, yeah?" you think to yourself. "Well watch this, fat man!"

As the ball arcs toward you, you prepare to whack one, secretly hoping that you will somehow make contact and carom one off that loud mouth third baseman's large and expanding forehead. You swing with everything you've got, and nearly fall down.

"Strike two!" says the umpire as the ball bounces two feet in front of home plate.

It's now that you know you're hosed. Your face feels flush as you realize that you are about to become the laughing-stock of the company. You have a vision of yourself getting fired and everyone in the company cheering as you're booted out the front door, carrying a cardboard box of your paltry belongings. Next, you envision your wife standing on the front porch of the house you two recently bought. She is weeping as a man pounds a BANK REPOSSESSION sign on your front lawn, which is brown because your water was shut off six weeks earlier.

As the pitcher starts her windup, you sigh—grateful that your wife wasn't feeling well enough to be at the game and to witness your demise.

You clear your head just in time to see the pitcher release the ball. As it floats toward you, everything slows down. As strike three approaches, you picture yourself and your wife living in a tent village on the banks of a cement aqueduct that carries the city's sludge out to sea. Oh, well, you think. You always dreamed of having a place right on the water.

A disheveled, toothless man walks by, and you ask if you can borrow a match to light a can of Sterno. It's your birthday and your wife wants to heat you up a two-week-old donut she found in a dumpster behind the police station. But he says, "No way! I ain't giving squat to the loser who struck out with the bases loaded!"

And then, the ball is almost upon you. You close your eyes and swing. And amazingly, you feel something hit your bat. Then you hear cheers coming from your team-mates, and you open your eyes just in time to see the ball lofting toward left field. You drop your bat and run as fast as you can, spurred on by your imaginary toothless neighbor, who's right on your heels with a flaming tiki torch.

The other team's chiseled left fielder, who—rumor has it—was once drafted by the Pittsburgh Pirates, races for the ball. "Oh, no!" you think. He actually has a chance to catch it. He dives and extends his arm . . . *thunk!* The ball lands squarely in his glove. You can't believe your bad luck. You could've been a hero! It could have meant a promotion! A bigger house! That German-made two-seat Roadster you've been eyeing! But now, nothing but stale dumpster donuts.

And then, as Mr. All-Star hits the ground, the ball pops loose. Your team goes crazy! One run scores! Two runs score! As your teammates spill from the dugout, you stand on first base, not totally sure of what just happened. You see them rushing to you, and for a split second you fear that you might be in for a public flogging. But you soon figure it out when they hoist you onto their shoulders and carry you around the infield, shouting your name. "Grimsky!" Grimsky!" they chant.

Dang, you wish your wife were here.

Later, after pizza and beer, the check comes; but you're not allowed to throw in so much as a nickel. "Heroes don't pay!" your boss says.

You haven't received this many pats on the back since your junior year of high school, when you figured out how to hack into your chemistry teacher's computer to give all your friends a sneak peek at the midterm.

You get home around six, bursting to tell your wife every detail of your heroics. But when you walk in, the first thing you see is the dining table set for two. The candles are lit and the lights are low. The evening reeks of romance.

"Oh, no," you think, as you check today's date on your iPhone. It's not your anniversary, her birthday, the date you got engaged, or even the anniversary of your first date together. So what's the deal?

"Hi, sweetie," your wife says as she comes out of the kitchen. She is wearing a slinky dress and looks even more spectacular than usual.

"Hi," you answer tentatively. "Wow," you say, indicating the table. "What's up?"

"Oh, nothing," she says with an impish smile. "I just thought we'd have a nice, quiet dinner at home. You OK with that?"

"You bet," you say, giving her a big kiss.

"So how was the game?"

You tell her the whole story . . . except the part about your first two at-bats and that the opposing pitcher's name was Jenny. After you finish, she throws her arms around your shoulders and says, "My hero." Then she follows that with an amazingly long and tender kiss.

You determine that the night might be full of amazing possibilities, so perhaps a shower is in order.

What a guy.

Later, you two have just finished your salad when your wife says casually, "Sooooo . . . you remember Jim and Nina's wedding?"

"Remember? Of course; it was only a month ago."

"Actually, it's been five weeks," she says with a smile.

"OK," you say, studying her for any hint of where this may be going.

"And do you remember what we did after the reception?"

Of course you remember. Every detail. Who could forget a night like that? "Gee, no," you say sarcastically. "Exactly what was it we did again?"

She laughs.

"I'll always remember that night," you say.

"Oh, I think we both will. . . ." she says, getting out of her chair and sitting on your lap. Then you notice a touch of moisture in her eye as she adds a word to the end of that sentence. It's a big word; a real big word. ". . . Daddy," she concludes.

"Daddy?" you repeat in your head. Did your wife just call you "Daddy?"

You look at her and she nods with a huge, beautiful smile on her face.

"You mean. . .?" you stammer.

"Yep," she says. "Congratulations." At least that's what you *think* she said, because she cried the last word.

You are simultaneously ecstatic and stunned; over the past few months you two have talked about starting a family; you both have good jobs and job security, especially since that left fielder didn't hold onto the ball. But you didn't think it would happen so soon. Are you really ready to be a dad? Are you up to the task? After thinking about it for a nanosecond, the answer is a resounding "Yes!"—which you scream as you lift your wife and spin her about the room. Then, when you remember that she is now a pregnant woman, you gently place her on the sofa and pepper her with questions. "Are you sure? Do you feel all right? Should we turn the guest bedroom into the baby's room?" And, of course, the old male standby: "Can we still have sex?"

She laughs and begins by saying that she's suspected it for a week or more, so today she picked up two home pregnancy kits at the pharmacy. Both were positive. But just to be sure, she called her sister, who's an ob-gyn doctor. They met at her office, and there's no doubt about it—she is 100 percent pregnant. You laugh, and cry, and cheer, and scream; then you take her in your arms and the two of you make out like it's 11:55 PM and you're two teenagers with a midnight curfew.

Later, you each call your parents with the news. Everyone is thrilled.

Later still, you and your wife decide to go to bed a little earlier than usual and continue the celebration.

At midnight, you watch her sleep next to you. You have never been happier. Your mind is going a mile a minute, and there's no way you can sleep, so you tiptoe out of the bedroom and grab your laptop. Sitting at the kitchen table, you smile when you think of all the wonderful things that lie ahead. Then, when you think about what all those wonderful things will cost, your smile fades and you go online and transfer some money from your savings into a new account you call simply, "Our Baby."

"What a day!" you think to yourself. In recalling the softball game, you wonder what would have happened if you had you struck out. Would it have had an impact on your job? Probably not. But then again, maybe.

You know you dodged a bullet today, and that next time you might not be so lucky, so you go out into the garage and find the crutches you got when you hurt your knee skiing. If you wrap your ankle just right, and hobble into work Monday morning, it just might do the trick.

"What's wrong, Grimsky?" your boss will ask, alarmed.

"I screwed up my ankle at the game Saturday," you say, trying to wince with just the right amount of pain, while still maintaining your image as a "hero." So you add, "I hurt it in the second inning . . . way before I got my hit."

"And you kept playing on it?" your boss says, full of admiration.

"Yessir, I did. Anything for the team. But the bad news is, it'll keep me out of action for awhile."

"How long?"

"The rest of the season," you answer with as much regret as you can fake.

Your boss takes the news hard, but still commends you for your spirit. When you get back to your office, you wonder if you did the right thing.

Of course you did. Like it or not, you've got to be more cautious now. After all, you're going to be a dad.

TWO

FROM PETER PAN TO PREGNANCY SUIT

OK, so you're going to be a father. You have engaged in a beautiful, selfless act to help bring a new life into this world. You muse that because of your willingness to part with your obviously brawny sperm, you may have co-created a child who could very well grow up to be a doctor who will find cures for the world's most devastating diseases. Or a statesman whose intelligence, compassion, and general amiability will allow her to build the bridge to world peace. Or an astral explorer who will find intelligent life on Mars. Or on Venus. Or on Fox News.

And even though your wife is only at the beginning of her pregnancy, you are so excited about your impending fatherhood that you are already mentally rearranging the house and socking away a little extra cash each week for college tuition, even though your little genius will likely be on full scholarship from kindergarten on.

When you look at your wife, you see the most beautiful woman in the world, full and ripe and almost beatific. You are suddenly fascinated by the cycle of birth and the rejuvenation of the species. You get misty-eyed at *The Lion King,* and yesterday, driving to work, you had to pull over and sob when an oldies station played "Daddy's Home."

But the only person you can share your feelings with is your wife, because if you ever mentioned any of these emotions to your single guy friends, you know they would ride you mercilessly.

"Jeez, grow a pair," you can hear one of them saying.

"Yeah," says another, handing you his cell phone. "If you want to talk about that crap, call Oprah."

And then, when the waitress comes for drink orders, they'd get a huge laugh out of ordering beers and Jäger-meister shots for themselves and an appletini for you.

You chalk this up to them still being little boys, caught in the Peter Pan syndrome. They're still irresponsible, delin-quent, bachelor playboys—able to drink, smoke cigars, and watch *Cops* and UFC fights whenever they want. They can buy all the skis and putters they want to.

Whew, you're glad you're not like that anymore, right? Right?!

An expectant mom, on the other hand, has a built-in support group and fan club throughout her pregnancy. Before she's even showing, just listen to the decibel level rise when she tells a group of her friends that she's pregnant. You haven't heard grown women scream like that since last time you were in Vegas and Tom Jones tossed a pair of his Fruit of the Looms into the crowd. Her friends will fawn over her and throw her an unending stream of baby showers. And once her pregnancy becomes more obvious, strangers in elevators will smile at her and say she has "a certain glow" about her.

You just stand by and smile proudly, as if to say, "And I'm the guy who made all of this possible."

But before you nominate yourself for Husband of the Year, you should also remember that you are also the man responsible for blessing your gorgeous wife with nine months of nausea, bloating, and so much extra tonnage that they won't even allow her on the truck scales alongside the interstate. She will also have you to thank for her dry hair, her swollen feet, and an emotional state that makes her go from high to low, from happy to sad, quicker than you can say "Dr. Phil."

And because of this emotional rollercoaster that your wife is experiencing, it is wise for you to go along with whatever she says. You need to remember that a pregnant woman has so many things going on in her body that during her pregnancy her emotional wiring can misfire at any time. And when it does, you need to be ready for it. With a smile.

"Honey, I think we should paint the baby's room mauve with persimmon highlights, don't you?" she says in her third month of pregnancy.

"Perfect," you say. "Except we just painted it yellow two weeks ago."

"What are you saying? That I made a mistake?"

"No way! Mauve and persimmon it is."

"Great," she says. "Can you do it tomorrow?"

"Tomorrow?" you blurt. "I was gonna play golf tomorrow."

"Golf?" she roars. "You'd actually go out and hit a ball around when you could be here doing something nice for your child. OK, fine, go! I'll call my father and ask him to do it."

"Whoa," you say. "Weren't you listening? I said I *was* gonna play golf. But that was before I knew I'd have the opportunity to do some painting." Then you wrap your arms around her and give her a big kiss. "Thanks, honey," you say. "I am so glad we're pregnant."

"WE?" OK, Nancy Boy, hold it right there. This sounds like the same "we" you use when you watch your home-town team on television and get all puffed up at the end of the game, yelling, "We won! We won!" Look, pal, let us shine the harsh light of reality on this. *They* won. You didn't do anything except watch from the couch wearing your underpants. You saying, "We're pregnant!" is like your wife saying, "*We've* got jock itch!"

So make no mistake that when it's baby time, your wife will be doing all the heavy lifting. And as her pregnancy progresses, you will learn that your role as "equal partner" has been temporarily suspended, and you are now reduced in rank to cheerleader, general factotum, and support team leader. Your wife is now Cher to your Sonny, Cleopatra to your Marc Antony, Madonna to your cabana boy.

And if you have even the slightest doubt about this, you will come to your senses when your wife enthusiastically enrolls the two of you in birthing class or lessons in Lamaze, natural childbirth, low-impact water birthing, or "Magic Midwifery." Or, as many old-school husbands (not you, of course) refer to it: "That stupid thing I have to go to on Tuesday nights." We know that some guys can't get rid of the nagging feeling that these classes are nothing but a plot by militant feminists to rub our noses in the steaming pile of trouble we've caused by forcing our unnatural lust on innocent, virginal women. We probably inherited this attitude from past generations . . . like maybe from our own dads.

"Hey, Jimmy," your father says to you over the phone. "Listen, I have a couple of tickets for the hockey game Tuesday night. How 'bout you and I . . ."

"Shoot, Dad, I'd love to. But I'm busy Tuesday."

"You can't move it? I thought we'd head out early; have dinner at Marco's Meat Palace."

"Sounds great, Dad, but it's something I just can't get out of."

"Something for work, eh?"

"No. Tuesday night is our first birthing class."

There is a moment of silence, and then you hear your dad pounding his phone's receiver onto his kitchen counter. This is one of his favorite bits, and you've seen him perform it hundreds of times over the years. As you wait for the banging to stop, you know exactly what his next words will be: "I'm sorry, but my phone must be broken. What the hell'd you say?"

"Birthing class, Dad. Marsha and I are going for the next six weeks."

"*Birthing* class," he bellows. "What the devil are you going to do there?"

"Uh, Dad . . . Marsha's pregnant. You remember hearing something about that?"

"Don't be a wiseacre. Why is Marsha dragging *you* along?"

"She's not dragging me, Dad; I want to go so I can help support her."

"Support her? What? You don't go to work every day?"

"During the delivery, Dad. I want to learn how to help her with breathing, relaxing . . . things like that. That's what dads do these days."

"Oh, well excuse me, Mr. Bill Cosby! Jimmy, how many brothers and sisters do you have?"

"Six," you sigh, wondering how he's going to use this against you.

"And do you know how many of you kids I saw born because I was in there helping your mother breathe? Zero! Nada! Zippo! I was out where I was supposed to be . . . in the waiting room, smoking cigarettes with the other schmucks who were going through the same thing I was!" Then he takes a pause to catch his breath. "Breathing . . ."

he repeats with disbelief. "Marsha's been breathing pretty good for twenty-nine years now, don't you think? She can't get along for an hour or so without you?"

"Dad . . ."

"Aw, never mind. I'll ask one of your brothers to go to the game with me. But I'll give you a call if I ever get tickets to the Ice Capades."

And that's that.

But in reality, birthing classes give a man an up close and personal understanding of the entire process. The first thing you'll learn is that it's much easier—and certainly more fun—to put babies in than it is to get them back out. You will see the sacrifices your wife makes, whether it's denying herself worldly pleasures, or undertaking an exercise regimen that would challenge a Navy SEAL. Hey, hotshot, you think you have it tough? Try taking morning sickness out for a spin! Or how about lugging around an extra fifty pounds in the dead of summer? Or try lumbering through a mall on feet swollen to the size of Ronald McDonald's shoes, wearing an empathy suit.

There's no doubt about it: expectant moms demonstrate the kind of zeal and commitment rarely seen outside a monastery.

So, by the time you near your final class, you will be a natural metronome for your wife's breathing. You will have learned more than you ever wanted to know about Braxton Hicks contractions, although you've become an unabashed fan of Kegel exercises. You've heard the terms *colostrum* and *meconium* enough to know that they are not something you find at the beach with a metal detector. And you've even come up with some killer episiotomy jokes that will certainly amuse everyone in the delivery room except, perhaps, your wife.

As each of your fellow dads-to-be due date approached, you've watched them dash off for their birthing experience, and wondered how you and your wife will do when your time comes. All of a sudden, the thought of chain-smoking with your dad in the waiting room is not sounding all that crazy.

But you recover and dutifully place the packed bag by your front door. You've gone over every conceivable eventuality, and you've even rehearsed what you'll say to the cop who pulls you over for speeding, with your wife writhing in labor next to you.

And there's probably one other thing you've done that your wife may or may not know about . . . you've purchased a brand-new video camera to record every glorious moment of the birth of your wonder child.

Hold it right there! You need to pay close attention to what we are about to tell you. First, take a deep breath. Second, take the video camera out of the bag by the door put it in your closet. But keep the batteries charged for the christening, bris, ear piercing, or whatever ritual you've decided to subject your little prince or princess to.

You do not want to take a video camera into the delivery room. Why? Well, do you remember your high school driver's ed class, where you were forced to watch the goriest and grisliest highway patrol footage of body parts strewn all over the highway? Good. Now, exactly how many copies of those films do you keep in your video library to enjoy at your leisure?

Just as we thought: you wouldn't watch a film like that today, even if the alternative were going hunting with Dick Cheney.

Plus, do you really think your wife will want you recording every excruciating and intimate detail of birth?

No way, particularly since she knows your aptitude with all things mechanical.

Just as the baby starts to emerge, you yell, "Cut!"

The doctor looks at you, dumbfounded.

"Would you mind sticking the little fella back in?" you ask. "I was out of focus."

Trust us; we've talked to a lot of foolish dads who thought their child's birth would make for some fine viewing later on. Not a single one of them has ever looked at it; although one of our dad friends mistakenly lent his video to his next-door neighbor's seven-year-old because it had somehow been mislabeled *Lilo and Stitch*. These once-cordial neighbors are no longer speaking, even though our friend offered to pay for half of the child's therapy.

So although you will make the right decision and leave the video camera at home, you will not be able to resist shooting some stills with your cell phone. But once serious labor begins, what is lost in still shots is the running invective that will begin spewing from your wife's mouth. You can't believe that this is the woman you've known as being so even-tempered and gracious. The same woman who you thought might wear white gloves and an Easter hat throughout the process suddenly begins calling you names that reflect poorly on your mother's virtue and marital status at the time of your birth, and remarks on how she'd like to permanently separate you from your penis.

So no matter how many cell phone shots you take, the only that will ever see the light of day is the one where your wife—drenched and exhausted after going through the most demanding physical experience possible—is holding your one-minute-old baby.

"Smile, honey," you say.

And smile she will. But if you study the photo more closely, you will see that behind the smile lies an expression that says, "If you take one more picture of me looking like this, I will shove that cell phone somewhere where removing it will allow you, too, to experience the pain of childbirth."

Don't say we didn't warn you.

And finally, there is one other thing you should be prepared for in the delivery room: the medical staff—doctor, nurse, whoever else happens to be there—will casually talk about all sorts of things, apparently unaware and unconcerned that two people are about to experience a life-changing event.

I learned this firsthand. Minutes before our first child was born—while I was urging my wife to "Push!" and "Breathe," and she was swearing at me, the obstetrician and delivery nurse decided it was an excellent time to talk about sports, the weather, and hospital romances. Then, when the veins in my wife's neck began bulging as she grunted and strained to bring our child into the world, the doctor and nurse saw that our son's head had exited the birth canal. But instead of making his way into the world face first, he chose to lead with the back of his noggin—most likely keeping an eye out behind him to make sure he wasn't being followed. Seeing this, the doctor casually said , "Uh-oh, it looks like another conehead."

Conehead?! I was aghast at the man's insensitivity! But when I peered over the doctor's shoulder to get a better look, I saw a perfect miniature of Dan Aykroyd's old character from *Saturday Night Live.* All the breath left my body, and a rush of images flooded my mind; most prominent was a picture of the Elephant Man, an eyehole cut out of his canvas hood, bitterly proclaiming, "I am a human being!"

Was this the life my son would be condemned to, just because of a few peyote buttons his father consumed back in the day? God, I would never forgive myself.

But as the doc cheerfully placed the baby, cord still attached, on Mom's suddenly deflated stomach, he turned to me and said, "Don't worry, Mr. Lynch; their little heads are so soft that they change shapes while trying to exit their mom. The swelling will be gone shortly."

The rush of relief was so great and immediate that I almost hugged him; but I decided that mom and baby should be the first ones to get that treatment. So after I checked my pants for mishaps, I threw my arms around them both. And then a few moments later, just as the doctor said, my son's head began to resemble that of every other human being born on this planet since the Ice Age.

So when your little bun pops out of the oven, try to remember that strained smile you tried to control when your wife first told you she was pregnant. When you hold your newborn for the first time, you'll see that your smile was for real. And take our word for it: it'll keep getting bigger and bigger every day.

THREE

ROUND, ROUND, ROUND, ROUND, I GET AROUND...

(Or at Least I *Used* To)

OK, so now it's official; you're a dad. Congratulations, and welcome to a club that's unlike any other. Whereas many groups have an official handshake or fist bump, dads have the head scratch, as in, "What just happened?" Your first few months in your new role will be a time of wonder, a time of amazement, a time of asking yourself, "How come my wife knows so much about this stuff and I don't know squat?" Don't lose any sleep over this, because you now have a little person in your life who will do a fine job of keeping you awake for the next thirty years or so.

Besides, why worry about something you can't change? You need to accept the fact that moms are generally better at this game than we are, and that the first two years are for what Mother Nature intended them to be: her way of bitch slapping you with the message, "Look, Mister Man, we know you're used to being in charge. But just chill out and we'll call you when we need you." (Warning: Do not let your wife see this! If she walks in while you're reading this page, rip it out and eat it.)

But this is not to suggest that you are not an integral piece of the family puzzle. On the contrary, you need to be constantly ready to jump into action when called upon.

You are the firefighter to the battalion chief; the bull pen to the starting pitcher; the Pips to Gladys Knight.

But what dad training have you really had? Oh, sure, you went to the birthing classes we've already talked about, but those focused on how to help *before* your baby was born. And besides, you didn't catch every word the instructor said, because you had your earpiece in, listening to the hockey game. But now that your toothless tax deduction has officially arrived, what's your next step? Well, here are a few operating instructions to help you through your first two years.

PRACTICE YOUR FALSETTO

Because newborns seem to respond better to high pitches, you'll need to work on training your voice to move up a few octaves when you're trying to communicate with your baby. While your natural, manly baritone may be perfect for things like, "Out?! Jeez, ump, open your eyes!" and "Fore!" its deepness is likely to frighten your child when you say things like, "Here comes the tickle monster!" or, "Poo-poo again? That's my little man!"

If you have trouble developing a "baby voice" of your own, there are plenty of high-pitched folks you can listen to and imitate. Like your Aunt Harriet, when she calls her cats in for dinner; or one of your mom's Johnny Mathis albums; or any interview with Mike Tyson.

LEARN TO CREEP

Yeah, we know that you think walking on your tiptoes is kind of unmanly, but hey, carrying a dirty diaper at arm's length with one hand while you hold your nose with your other isn't exactly *Rambo* material either. You've already observed that newborn babies are fine with soothing sounds, but very sensitive to jarring ones, which you attribute to your wife putting the iPod on her stomach and playing all that calming Mozart music while she was pregnant. You're convinced that your baby would be able to sleep through a tractor pull if she'd thrown a little AC/DC on there.

Anyhow, with a light-sleeping baby in your life, you will have to learn to slink about your house like a cat burglar, because there's nothing worse than finally getting your baby back to sleep in the middle of the night, laying her gently in her crib, and then waking her with your plodding footsteps as you leave her room. A good way to avoid such a mistake is to wear heavy socks and "ice skate" out of her room after you put her down. Although this works very well on wood floors, you need to use caution if her room has a thick carpet. The electrostatic you create might cause a loud *zap* when you touch her doorknob. And if this sudden sound doesn't wake your finally sleeping beauty, then your stream of obscenities—several of which cast aspersions on your mother—certainly will.

AVOID OVERCONFIDENCE

You're getting cocky because now you can fold up the playpen, car seat, and travel crib easier than you can fold a pair of boxers. You've totally figured out those changing tables that have begun popping up in men's restrooms of family-friendly restaurants and amusement parks. And just last week you mastered the technique of unfastening a pair of OshKosh B'gosh overalls with just one hand, which made you wish you'd developed such dexterity fifteen years earlier, when you had that humiliating experience with Mary Elizabeth Curley and her double-snap Maidenform.

You're also adept at handling a baby wipe with one hand while gingerly pinching two ankles together with the other. You've become proficient at loading the car for a trip—even a short one—knowing that it's akin to going on a safari, and that it requires the logistical planning of a space shuttle launch. Diaper bag? Check. Pacifier? Check. Cash? Check. Yep, you reason, you've got this whole baby thing figured out.

But be careful, Mr. Father Knows Best, because just when you think you're totally in sync with the whole dad/baby dynamic, you'll be thrown a curveball you didn't see coming. And it's likely to hit you right between the eyes. Or the legs.

This curveball is called teething, which is a baby's way of saying to you, "Well, if I'm not going to sleep all night, then neither are you!" The first sign that your baby might be going through this painful but unpreventable phenomenon is an almost constant drooling. Then, you'll notice that the diapers are runnier than usual. If, however, you miss these two signs, you will soon be alerted by your baby's constant screaming at a pitch and volume that will set off your car alarm.

Your baby will be so inconsolable that she won't even fall for the old peek-a-boo trick, which has been your go-to maneuver whenever things get tough. Although it's heartbreaking for you to see your little one going through such discomfort, it's equally frustrating because there doesn't seem to be anything you can do to help. Your father suggests rubbing bourbon on the little one's gums, but bourbon is your father's solution for every ailment, from snakebites to sciatica. Besides, if anyone needs bourbon, it will be you.

After a week or so, the crying will diminish as your baby's "toofies" or "teefers" push through her gums to make their appearance. Then she will begin sleeping through the night once more, meaning that you will no longer suffer the embarrassment of dozing off during early morning business meetings. Even the ones you were conducting.

So you rode out the trauma of teething and you're now back to your cocky self. Then, one fall Monday evening you settle in your favorite chair, waiting for the Jets–Patriots game to start. Your wife is at the gym and you are in charge of the baby, who is playing on the blanket that you spread out on the floor right next to your chair. You want to introduce her to the whole football experience so she doesn't grow up being a girly-girl who doesn't know the difference between a touchdown and goose down. As the teams prepare for kickoff, you reach down to lift her onto your lap.

Ohmigod! Where is she? You get your answer soon enough when you see her cute little rear end scurrying under your computer table. Whoa, she's started crawling! When you stand and proudly call her name, she looks back at you, a big smile on her face—a smile that says, "Hey, this is fun! I should have tried this a long time ago!" You, on the other hand, think to yourself, "This is so exciting!"

But your excitement over her ability to self-transport will wane as she becomes more agile and mobile. This is because she will also become more hostile when you try to prevent her from going places. You will long for the days when she was just a doorstop beneath your kitchen table, the days when you could go out to your favorite Mexican restaurant and she would fall asleep in her snuggly, her tiny head resting on your chest, splattered with salsa.

Your house will begin to look like it's been ransacked . . . chairs and tables turned over on their sides, blocking her path to danger areas. You will not be able to get into the kitchen for your morning coffee without having to hurdle an overturned end table or pole vault a dining room chair. All electrical outlets, cabinets, and drawers will be battened down and secured as though you lived in a double-wide trailer smack in the middle of Tornado Alley.

And then, just when you think you have every possible danger covered, your daughter will crawl over to the overturned coffee table and pull herself up. You watch this with a mixture of pride and horror, because you know that she is not far from accomplishing a feat that separates mankind from most other species . . . the ability to stand upright and walk.

And once your child gets past her first wobbly, drunken-sailor first steps, she will quickly learn that she can get from Point A to Point B faster than she could on her knees. And once she becomes even more surefooted, she also realizes that she can get there faster than you can, which is why most trouble is located at Point B. Because if a child could break something valuable at Point A, there'd be no reason to go to Point B in the first place.

It's at this stage that you will stow anything of value above waist level. Or better yet, store it in a closet until your eighteen-month-old dynamo leaves for college. All those cool Mexican artifacts on your coffee table? Box them safely in the garage. Your unopened coffee-table books and copies of *Architectural Digest*, there only to impress your friends? You can now use them to line the hamster cage.

Before long, your formerly hip living room—once so tastefully decorated with all sorts of cool things—will now resemble the set of *Sanford and Son*. With everything in your home sporting pabulum drool and padded corners, you wonder if the straitjacket can be far behind.

You will begin to wonder what happened to your life as you knew it. And pondering this mystery can lead you down a slippery slope of second-guessing yourself and your choices. This leads to our final instruction in the birth to two years phase.

KEEP A POSITIVE SELF-IMAGE

When you were single, you were probably like most young males of the species, who saw themselves as devil-may-care bad boys who relished their place on the fringe of society. In our minds, we were swashbuckling adventurers, able to do anything at any time. We all wanted to be that bad boy Alanis Morrissette sang about in "You Oughta Know."

Even after we were married—before children—we continued to hold onto the notion that there was still a little bit of outlaw in us. We lived on the edge; we pushed the envelope, even if the extent of our rebelliousness was nothing more than hanging a picture of a Harley in our bland cubicle at work; or wearing a Hawaiian shirt on casual Friday.

And then came baby.

At first, there were mixed signals. Whenever it was just you with your baby, women seemed to still be attracted to you, whether it was at the Laundromat, the supermarket, or the beach. At first, you took this as a testament to your inherent charm: like it or not, you've still got it. But it didn't take long for you to see the truth . . . that, because you have a baby, women feel comfortable around you because you are safe; you have been officially labeled "harmless." After all, you're a dad, a pillar of the community, a person of responsibility who undoubtedly has jumper cables in his trunk right now! And Handi Wipes in his glove box.

Still a bad boy, eh? Well guess what, Scarface? With your precious papoose asleep on your back, strapped into his BABYBJÖRN while you peruse the disposable diaper aisle at the supermarket, discount coupon in hand, you are the antithesis of bad . . . you are a dad!

And that is a good thing; it just takes some of us a while to realize it. My epiphany struck one afternoon after a family outing at a local amusement park. There I was, driving in the family Volvo wagon, my wife next to me, our two-year-old strapped into his safety seat in back, right alongside my mother-in-law. As I looked at myself in the mirror, I felt a cold blade stab at my heart as the realization set in: I had become my own worst nightmare! I had cuffs on my neatly pressed pants. I had a supermarket discount card. My car was as clean as my underpants. Shoot, I was actually wearing underpants! I had an insurance policy and a mortgage. I cast about in my mind, looking for some sort of loophole, but there was none. I had totally lost my edge. My song was no longer "You Oughta Know." It was "Twinkle, Twinkle Little Star." Oh, sure, I could still go out to happy hour whenever I wanted . . . provided it was at Chuck E. Cheese.

I found myself thinking about the future; and worse, the future extended beyond what I was doing that night. My God, I thought, how the mighty have fallen.

Then I pulled into our driveway, and while my wife and mother-in-law rounded up the diaper bag, the stroller, and assortment of fifty-cent stuffed animals that cost me about eighty bucks, I went to retrieve my sound-asleep two-year-old from his car seat. Unbuckling him, I smiled at the huge red ring around his mouth—a souvenir from a cherry snow cone. Then, as I lifted his limp body from the seat and held him to me, he wrapped his chubby little arms around my neck and held me as tightly as he could.

Then, as he buried his face in the crook of my neck and let loose a contented snore, I could tell that he was exactly where he wanted to be.

And from that moment on, "Twinkle, Twinkle Little Star" was plenty fine with me.

FOUR

THE THEORY OF RELATIVITY

So you're beginning to feel like you just might be settling in to this whole "rad dad" thing, and hope that some day you might just have it all down pat. Of course, there's no way that will ever happen, but it's not a bad target to shoot for. Will you ever hit the bull's-eye? Probably not, but if you can make it through the game without burying a dart in someone's skull, you've done just fine.

If, however, you foolishly begin brimming over with confidence in your dad skills, you'd be well advised to consider the qualifications needed to become a father in the first place: an occasionally functioning penis and the ability to make a human female laugh with your lame imitation of Cliff, the mailman on *Cheers*. And even though you can become a father with far fewer qualifications than it takes to drive a forklift or to install a toilet, you're sharp enough to realize that there's very little that can replace hands-on, in-the-trenches experience when it comes to being a dad. Like Woody Allen observed, "ninety percent of life is showing up." And people can say what they want about you, but they can't say you're not *there*.

So now, as you set out to truly hone your parenting skills, you will come face to face with, like it or not, one of the most profound truisms in all of parent-dom. The old African bromide says it best: "It takes a village to raise a child." In Western terms, this means that anyone and everyone who either has or has ever had a child, glimpsed a child, or who was ever a child themselves, will have a comprehensive list of dos and don'ts which they are only too happy to share with you. And while you are free to ignore most of this advice, there are some sources whom you absolutely must listen to, or at least pretend to.

GRANDPARENTS

They just might be the most critical source of all. Let's review the evidence. One set of your child's grandparents raised you, and if you must say so yourself, they did a totally admirable job, dotting all the *I*s and crossing all the *T*s. Just look at the way you turned out: you're tall (for your family, anyway); you're strong (see "tall"); you're secure, ("Hey, wait. Did I hear someone say I wasn't tall?"); you're a pillar of the community; and you're a dad and husband without peer. So you have to give some credibility to your parents' advice, simply because of their sterling track record. You feel the same way about your wife's parents, although to a lesser extent. After all, look at how stubborn she is. And what is she always grinning about, particularly when you get that serious tone in your voice? No, they dropped the ball there, but for the most part, they get honorable mention.

Oddly, when they first meet up with baby you hear almost identical sentiments from the grandparents. They'll usually exclaim something like, "What a beautiful baby! We hope he turns out to be the same kind of child for you as you were for us." At first you assume that this is the highest accolade, but as your baby gets older and begins to exhibit certain personality traits, you wonder if it wasn't some kind of grandparent payback curse. Still, there is one thing about which you can be absolutely certain: grandparents are a gift from God. They understand from day one that they were put here on this earth to spoil your child, and they are well on their way to receiving a "mission accomplished" in that category. Being a grandparent must be the best job in the world, as they get all the advantages of raising children and none of the drawbacks, and if you're lucky enough to have any grandparents around while raising your child, you will soon learn to value them like precious gems. They can generally be depended on to be last-minute babysitters, purveyors of child-rearing wisdom, and unabashed cheerleaders for everything your child does. They often act as the voice of reason, gently reminding you of your own childhood foibles.

They can, however, also take a cynical view of some parenting trends and terminology that weren't around when they were raising you.

Let's say your father stops by unannounced one Saturday afternoon to see if he can take your seven-year-old son out for some ice cream.

"Oh, sorry, Dad," you say, "but Lester isn't home; he's at a playdate."

"A what?" he asks.

"A playdate with Timmy."

"Timmy?" he asks. "Isn't he that chubby little redhead kid who lives next door?"

"Yes," you say, then reverse yourself. "I mean, no. We don't refer to Timmy as *chubby*. We say that he's a little bit bigger than Lester."

"A little bit? Shoot, he's bigger than two Lesters." Then he thinks for a minute. "But I still don't get this playdate thing. Since Timmy lives right next door, why doesn't Lester just run over there, knock on his door, and say, 'Hey, big guy . . . want to play?'"

"That's not the way things are done these days, Dad," you tell him.

"Why not? Worked fine for you and Charlie Ruble."

"Look, Dad, it's just the way we choose to do it. If Lester went over without a playdate scheduled, what if Timmy was busy? Lester could feel rejected."

Your father stares at you for a moment. "You're yanking my chain, right?"

You assure him you're not, and he just shakes his head and leaves.

A few hours later, he phones your house. "Hello, Son. Listen, I'd like to talk to Lester. Or do I need a phone date first?" He cackles at his humor, and this time *you* are the one left shaking your head.

But overall, grandparents offer wise and dispassionate advice when you are forced to deal with the hysterical opinions from other members of the "village." They can be an invaluable source of advice, comfort, and sympathy, particularly when you find yourself reaching for that bottle of Prozac.

BROTHERS

You know that your brother—particularly if he's your *younger* brother (see chapter eight for more on this)—has been patiently waiting to get even with you ever since you put Tabasco in the Super Soaker. You also know you should have probably left his baseball card collection alone, but who knew he'd make such a fuss over the moustache and eyeglasses you drew on his stupid 1961 Roger Maris? And you obviously knew nothing good would come of your putting the Ben-Gay inside his jock strap before the city cross-country finals. But hey, you thought, what's he gonna do about it? You're older and bigger than he is.

Well, now that you're a dad, he knows that you're ripe for the picking. So enjoy a cold serving of revenge, Pilgrim.

Payback can start as early as your wife's pregnancy. For example, your little brother could call Dad and suggest he invite you to a hockey game Tuesday night, even though your brother knows full well that you have a birthing class scheduled. That'd be hilarious; Dad would never let you hear the end of that.

Christmastime and your child's birthday also offer excellent opportunities for your little brother to even the score. For example, on your child's first birthday, good ole Uncle Steve may present him with a loud, battery-powered train engine, complete with a whistle and "choo-choo" device that makes your neighbors think they are living in Grand Central Terminal. The following Christmas, your brother is almost guaranteed to give your child a drum set before the soft spot on his head grows together. (The baby's head, not your brother's. His will never completely form.)

It will also be Uncle Steve who will take it as his responsibility to pass on scatological "guy culture" to your nine-year-old son, or to impress upon your daughter the need for extreme caution in her future relationships with males. Every family has one of these uncles. If he's single, he's the guy who shows up at any family function with a Hooters waitress on his arm. He laughs too much and too loudly, which makes him a favorite with the little ones, whom he always greets with a soft left hook to the belly, taking a prizefighter's stance to do so. There will be a lot of yelling, either to poke fun at good behavior or to interrupt one of your stories to present the true (his) version. He will make an early but noisy departure, pressing dollar bills into the hands of his nieces and nephews and saying that he's got another function to get to—one that he says will be attended by a famous actor, comedian or musician . . .

always someone who is extremely popular with the younger set. He will promise to get autographed photos for anyone who wants one, but will show up at the next gathering without any pictures and a story about how he had to punch out Johnny Depp because he refused to sign them.

On the other hand, if Uncle Steve is married—which he often is—it is entirely possible that his wife escaped from prison, a nuthouse, or a pimp. He will have coached her to treat you with contempt, dredging up old family stories that validate your incompetence, as well as to make fun of your penny loafers.

If you visit him where he lives, it is likely that he is house-sitting. Yet he will make no bones about showing off all the cool stuff the home's owner has accumulated and will somehow give the impression that the owner's success is entirely dependent on his friendship with Uncle Steve.

But the worst part will only take place if your knuckle head brother is somehow allowed to procreate. His parenting skills will be a reflection of his outlook and lifestyle, because he seems intent on raising his own kids to become outlaw bikers or brooding sociopaths. But believe it or not, as your children grow into adults, they will learn valuable coping skills as a result of Uncle Steve and his kids. They will probably be able to look back on these precious family get-togethers with fondness, and might even be able to recount them with wry amusement when writing to their cousins in the penitentiary.

SISTERS

The difference between having brothers and sisters is as elementary as the difference between male and female. If you have a sister, you'll understand what this means. For one thing, "Auntie" won't let your baby's feet touch the ground until the child is three years old. Your sister will just not allow this to happen! Whereas your brother wants to pose your infant daughter in a John Deere cap with a beer in front of her and a cigarette in her mouth, your sister can stare into the baby's eyes in wordless wonder for hours on end. Your sister will volunteer to bathe the baby, babysit the baby, and she will even drop everything to change a diaper. You will begin to wonder if you ever knew your sister in the first place. Is this the same person who tattled on your every misstep as a child? The same person who taught you your first curse word and then ratted you out for using it? You bet she is! What's more, you find that your sister-in-law is the same way. The very same person who rode her broomstick to your house morphs into Mary Poppins when she's around the kids. She still looks at you with the same expression that she uses when she finds something distasteful on the soles of her UGGs, but it's nice to know that when she's away from her coven, she can be almost civil.

Nieces and nephews seem to instinctively understand that they can tell an aunt things they would never consider telling Mom. And it doesn't matter whether Aunt Sue is single or married. Whereas you would never entertain the preposterous notion of leaving your child with your single brother—maybe in the event of a global apocalypse, and you and your wife have been swept away by tidal waves— your single sister is not only responsible but she invites the opportunity to help. While you can't count the times your brother has gotten the kids riled up, filled them with junk food, and then blithely departed just as the sugar is pushing them to near delirium, your sister seems to have a calming effect on the kids. Aunts will actually sit and play with their nieces and nephews, offer advice on their problems, and some have been known to carry on actual conversations where, get this, they *listen* to your kids! The only possible speed bump is that you are not allowed to register shock or surprise when your young child spends the night with a single aunt and returns home with questions about sexual harassment, condoms, or why all men are bastards.

COUSINS

At family gatherings, cousins are usually the bird crap in the cheese dip. They come in a dazzling variety of permutations, and rarely are any of them benevolent. As discussed, cousins take their cues from their parents, which means they are likely the children of your younger brother. These cousins seem to enjoy passing on their parents' version of family lore and legend, in which you are generally portrayed as somewhere between a clown and a loser. Cousins often impose your obvious shortcomings on your children, which means that even though your child is in honor classes, plays a varsity sport, and heads up the mock trial team, the cousin with the black fingernails, Megadeth T-shirt, and sealed criminal file somehow feels vastly superior.

During family gatherings, you must be aware of the cousin dynamic at all times. If your jungle gym that has survived twelve years suddenly turns up thrashed; or if a fire of mysterious origin breaks out; or if valuable heirlooms turn up lost or broken, always look to the cousins. But there's an interesting corollary to this rule: Bear in mind that your own children can be cousins too, and all that that implies. If you see signs of antisocial or destructive behavior in your children, you must be hard but fair.

After all, what do you expect from cousins?

FIVE

TEACH YOUR CHILDREN WELL

Because well over 60 percent of mothers with young children work outside the home, the odds are pretty fair that you are married to one of these mothers. Let's say your wife is on a six-week maternity leave, and your company provided you with seven days of paternity home time when your baby was born; but unfortunately, that was the same week your mother-in-law flew in from New Jersey to help your wife, and the two of you have never been particularly chummy. For one, she always prayed her little girl would marry "a nice, serious Italian Catholic boy." You, on the other hand, are an irreverent, red-haired, German-Irish who's investigating Buddhism. And you certainly didn't score any points with your mother-in-law at your wedding reception, when she overheard you telling your best man that her twin sister looked like Vito Corleone in a sundress.

You will hate going back to your job after that week off; the only bright spot will be dropping your mother-in-law at the airport on the way. The first several days back at work, you will call home every fifteen minutes to check on your wife and your new baby girl. And every night when you get home, you will swear that your daughter has grown at least an inch since you left that very morning.

These will be wonderfully exciting times that you hope will go on forever; but eventually your wife has to return

to work and you will have to select a day-care strategy for your child. And since she is barely a month old, your choices will be limited, because most preschools don't accept children less than one year of age. Your options will pretty much boil down to having someone come into your home to care for your child (HUGE dollars!), or dropping her off at someone else's home (BIG dollars!). Fortunately, your mom lives nearby, and she has volunteered to come over two days a week and watch the baby at your house (ZERO dollars!), which you think is a great idea. Your wife is thankful and accepts her gracious offer, but frets that she'll have to have the house spotlessly clean on the days your mother is coming. You'll try to put her mind at ease by saying that you'll be in charge of cleaning the house those days.

Your wife will laugh so hard she'll nearly wet herself.

Finally, after a lot of research, advice from other young parents, and a review of your financial situation, you decide that three days a week you will be dropping your precious baby at the home of "Miss Rita," a jocular, energetic woman in her early fifties whose house is as tidy as can be. Rita is a retired schoolteacher with pages of impeccable reference letters; and after seeing how she interacts with your baby, there is no doubt that she's far and away superior to every other place you checked out.

You're relieved you found Miss Rita; your wife, however, is absolutely ecstatic. She gushes to everyone about the loving day-care person you two found, and how your little Samantha will flourish under Miss Rita's tender nurturing. . .

. . . Until the night before she's scheduled to return to work.

"What if she's hiding something?" your wife says, bolting upright in bed.

"Huh? Who?" you mumble. You were just starting to fall asleep.

"Miss Rita," she says with a derisive sneer. "If that's her real name," she adds, oozing suspicion. "How do we know she's not really a Joan, or a Martha, or a Sadie?"

"Sadie?" you say, incredulous.

"Whatever," she says. "The point is, why doesn't she use her last name? Because she's hiding something."

"Burton," you remind her. "It's Rita Burton."

"That's what she *says* it is, but how do we *really* know?"

Before you use any word like *crazy* or *nuts*, you recall the article you read on postpartum depression. Your wife has exhibited absolutely none of the symptoms; in fact, if anyone has been depressed, it's you—thinking about how you have to sell your beloved Porsche because it's been deemed too small and too fast for a father to drive around with a new baby.

"Honey, you're talking crazy," you say. "We checked Rita out every which way . . . her references, she's licensed with the city, and what about Bill and Tina? Rita watched their baby for over two years. They're crazy about her."

"I've never liked Bill and Tina. Something very shifty about them," she says, grasping at straws.

"Sweetie," you start, having a pretty good idea of what's going on here. But she cuts you off.

"I think we moved too quickly on this. Maybe we should reconsider some of the people we ruled out."

"Like who? That lady who had more cats than teeth? Or maybe we should go with that twenty-three-year-old who lives next to the meatpacking plant. Yep, nothing

better than picking up our daughter every day and have her
smelling like beef shank. Or how about . . ."

But before you can lay any more thoughtless sarcasm on
her, your wife begins to cry softly.

"Nice going," you say to yourself. "What a jerk."

You take her in your arms and apologize. "Honey, it'll
be OK. Look, I wish we didn't have to take Samantha to
day care, too. But we agreed that we need two incomes . . .
at least until the economy picks up, right?"

She nods.

"Look, Rita's everything we could have asked for. You
said so yourself."

"I know, but . . ." she says.

"I understand how hard it's going to be for you tomorrow,
leaving Samantha for the first time."

She nods again, fighting back a sob.

"Tell you what; how about I go in to work a little late in
the morning? That way you can say good-bye to Samantha
here, and I'll take her to Miss Rita's."

"What?" she says. "Just dump her without her mom?"
There's no way that will happen, she tells you. Besides, she
made a long list of things about Samantha that Miss Rita
should be aware of. But then, she stops and stares at you, a
big, appreciative smile on her face.

"That was really sweet of you to offer," she says before
kissing you.

"Hey, I can be a really sweet guy when I want to," you
respond with a smile.

"Hmmmm," she says, grinning. "That's what my mom
told me before you took her to the airport."

"She did not!" you answer in disbelief.

"Yep," your wife insists.

You can't believe it. Your mother-in-law really said that? About you?

"Note to self," you say to your wife with a smile. "Next time mother-in-law visits, be sure to keep her away from the Chianti!"

The two of you share a much needed laugh and soon fall soundly asleep. The next morning when you drop off your child for her first day of childcare, Miss Rita has a small box of Kleenex ready. She is a wise woman.

Over the next twenty-four months, Miss Rita will provide loving, creative, and nurturing child care for you and your daughter.

And when you pick Samantha up at the end of her final day with Miss Rita, it's you who will provide the Kleenex.

★   ★   ★

But if you think finding a good day-care provider is a difficult task, just wait until you try to get your child into a decent preschool. Here's how it will likely shake out.

First, you'll need to get used to the fact that your child will be put on a waiting list. That's right—a waiting list. We're not talking about trying to score World Series tickets, or even the latest version of the iPhone. We're talking preschool. This will cause you to think back to when you were little. There was no scrambling for a few cherished spots in some special preschool; in fact, you didn't even call it preschool. It was called nursery school, a place where there were no waiting lists, no admissions interviews, and no exorbitant fees. Your first day, all you did was show up and five minutes later throw a tantrum when you realized that your mother was going home without you. But you quickly grew to love nursery school, because all you did was play games, take naps, sip refreshments, and sing silly songs.

It was just like your college fraternity days.

So imagine your surprise when you find out that many of today's new parents are putting their children on waiting lists for desirable preschools when the child is born . . . and often before. This is because many preschools have *pre*-preschools, which begin accepting children as young as two. So to get into your first choice of preschools (age three), you need to first get your child into their pre-preschool at age two. We've even heard of a preschool in Marin County, California—the womb of "what's new?"—that has opened a pre-pre-pre-pre-school, which accepts fertilized embryos, as long as they're potty trained and one of the parents has a killer recipe for organic bruschetta.

So your wife got your daughter on a waiting list and you receive a call that there's an opening. It's a very prestigious preschool with a pre-preschool, and your wife is thrilled. Your interview is the following Friday afternoon, and you, your wife, and your two-year-old daughter are required to be there. You will both have to take time off work; and on the way to the school, your wife pleads with you, "Please, don't be a smartass."

Yeah, right. Like that could happen.

After filling out your application form and attaching a check for $100 (nonrefundable, even if your child is rejected) you meet with the director of admissions, a serious young man who looks like he hasn't seen sunlight since the Reagan administration. You consider telling him that—in a nice way, of course—but suspect that he may not remember the Reagan administration.

As he scans your application, something odd catches his eye. "I see you both work," he says with surprise. It's as if you had listed yourselves as nudists.

"Is there something wrong with that?" you ask.

"Not at all," he says. "I think it's . . . admirable. I also think it's good to have all sorts of people represented here."

You look at your wife and she sees the anger brewing in your eyes. She pats your knee, as if to say, "No smartassing, remember?"

Then you look to your two-year-old, who sits on your wife's lap, happily picking her nose. The admissions guy makes a note of this behavior, and you suspect he attributes it to both parents working. "Poor little girl, without parental supervision, of course she's going to dig for gold in public."

After reviewing the rest of your application without incident, he gives you a perfunctory tour of the facilities, which include a state-of-the-art computer lab, a language center, and fully equipped fitness and athletic facilities. You wonder what the heck any of this has to do with your two-year-old, and fear that she may be in way over her head. At home, she uses your old computer keyboard to pound wooden pegs into her Playskool station; her language consists of about a hundred words in English, of which only thirty are decipherable to anyone but you and your wife. Although when it comes to athletics, she does know the difference between a touchdown and goose down.

After the tour, the young man walks you to your car and says you'll be hearing something soon. He shakes hands with both of you, then crouches and offers his hand to your daughter. "It was nice meeting you, Samantha," he says to her warmly.

So what does your daughter do to impress the man who could hold her entire future in his hands? She looks up at you and says, "I gaw make poo-poo!"

On the drive home, your wife says she thinks the interview went well. You're incredulous, saying that there's absolutely no chance of it.

"If she gets into that school, then I'm the Lone Ranger," you say.

But your wife is so certain of her position that she challenges you to a wager: if your daughter isn't accepted, she says, she will cook and serve you a seven-course meal wearing nothing but a lace apron.

"Deal!" you say, already planning the menu in your head.

"But if she *does* get in . . ." your wife says.

"Name it," you say; as if there were a chance of that.

Your wife ponders it for a moment. "Oh, I'll think of something."

"Take your time," you say confidently.

Two weeks later, you receive notification from the school.

The following weekend, you sit over a plate of perfectly prepared lamb chops, your drop-dead favorite. You sigh after taking a whiff of the mint jelly blending its aroma with the Dijon glaze. You take a bite; it's wonderful.

"Good?" your wife asks from across the table.

"Awesome." Then you lift your wine glass in a toast. "You look beautiful tonight," you tell her.

"Oh, you too," she says with a chuckle as she clinks glasses with you.

As you sip, your waiter approaches the table. "Is everything satisfactory?" he asks, suppressing a laugh when he looks at you for the hundredth time. This is because you are in one of the tiniest restaurants in your town, and you are dressed in a Lone Ranger outfit, complete with mask.

"Perfect," you say. Then, as he starts off, you call after him, "Could you make sure that Silver has plenty of oats?!"

The waiter laughs, and so do the people at the tables near yours. Oh, the things a dad has to go through when his daughter gets accepted to a good pre-preschool.

SIX

LET'S TALK ABOUT SEX

Cool off, horn dog; we don't mean *that* kind of sex. We're talking about gender; you know . . . the female XY chromosomes present in your daughter, or the XX chromosomes of your son; the biological wiring that makes the two genders so different. We know that some men, when they first find out that their wife is pregnant, harbor a small, secret hope that they will have a male child to carry on the family name. This is fine if your name is Smith, or Jones, or Granicki; but what if you have the misfortune of a surname like bin Laden, or Manson, or Turdleson? Really . . . what's to carry on?

But regardless of how much you might be hoping for a boy, you will forget all about that as soon as you hold your newborn daughter for the first time. From the second she first peers at you with her spectacular blue eyes, the two of you will begin a lifelong friendship and love affair.

But whether you have a baby boy or baby girl, a child's first two years are pretty much gender non-specific. That is, male and female children will generally have the same likes, dislikes, and maladies. They will poop the same, cry the same, and spit up in your shirt pocket the same. They will laugh the same, coo the same, and cost the same. And whether you have a son or a daughter, you will regard your child as the cutest, most intelligent, and best-behaved toddler on this or any other planet. There's one significant exception to this, however; experience has shown that little girls are often more likely to begin crawling and walking at an earlier age than boys. This head start in ambulation may explain why wives enjoy making us take long walks, dragging us through malls, and why they always seem to manage to scurry into the bathroom before we do.

For young children, it's usually between the ages of three and five that the genetic road begins to take different directions. In these years, little girls will begin to develop vivid imaginations, and they will play "pretend" for hours on end. And often they will want to play it with you . . . without warning.

"Hello, sir," your four-year-old daughter, Regina, might say to you one Sunday afternoon while you're watching the last two minutes of a very close football game.

"Hey, Gina," you say to her absently, eyes glued to the television.

"I'm not Gina," she says firmly. "My name's, ummm, LuAnn. What would you like for breakfast this morning?"

What? You glance at her and see that she is wearing one of your wife's aprons and is holding a legal pad and your Mont Blanc pen that she obviously pilfered from your briefcase.

"Breakfast?" you repeat, making a mental note to do a better job of hiding that pen from now on.

"Yes," Regina, er, LuAnn answers. "How do you want your eggs cooked?"

"Did I say I wanted eggs?" you ask, getting into it, but still managing to keep one eye on the television. Agh, interception! Game over.

"Sir!" she says petulantly. "You always have eggs when you come in here."

"Well then, LuAnn," you say, switching off the game, "you should remember how I like my eggs, shouldn't you?"

She frowns at this. "Daddy . . ." she says impatiently.

"Daddy?" you answer quickly. "Why are you calling me 'Daddy'? My name's Earl, remember?"

She smiles that beautiful smile and her eyes twinkle at your willingness to enter her imaginary world. "That's right! So, Earl, do you want your eggs, um . . ."

You can see her four-year-old mind searching for the word you say to the waitress when the family goes out for breakfast every weekend.

"Scribbled?" she finally says.

"Yes, scribbled is perfect," you say as she "writes" this on her order pad. You also order bacon, hash browns, and cantaloupe, which she records with the ease of a court reporter; then she disappears into the kitchen.

A few moments later, she returns with a small plate containing five Wheat Thins, a cluster of grapes, and a dollop of what appears to be horseradish.

"Here you are," she says as she proudly sets the plate in front of you. "Just the way you like it."

"Why thank you, LuAnn," you say, digging into your pocket. "And for such excellent service, I think you deserve a nice tip." You remove a quarter and hand it to her. "Here you go."

She is absolutely thrilled. She gives you a big kiss and says, "Thank you, Earl!" Then she turns and scampers toward the kitchen. "Mommy, Daddy gave me a dollar!"

You quickly turn the television back on. The game just ended and everyone is cheering wildly. "What an amazing finish!" the announcer says.

But you could care less as you dig into your feast of crackers and grapes.

Boys of this age, on the other hand, appear to lack the imagination needed to create such interesting parallel universes. That is why they seem to be limited to bopping each other over the head with anything handy. And learning the hilarity involved in making strange noises and aromas come from their bodies.

And it's also around this time that girls' natural mothering instincts will begin to surface, and they will begin playing with dolls: feeding them, bathing them, swaddling them.

Boys' nurturing instincts also begin showing themselves at this age, and are most often expressed by overfeeding the goldfish to death and trying to give the dog a haircut.

Girls of this age like to dress up pretty and wear new clothes and outfits, just like Mommy does.

Boys, however, tend to throw on whatever's handy, regardless if it matches . . . just like Daddy.

But don't let this apparent mother/daughter, father/son thing fool you. Because during this time a mother will start to form a special closeness with her son, and a father will do the same with his daughter. It just seems to be the nature of things, and perhaps explains why the expressions "Mommy's boy" and "Daddy's girl" came into being.

In the ages between six and eight, you will see even more disparities between the two genders. For one, these are the years girls begin to develop logic and the ability to think things out; in other words, this is when they reach the "age of reason."

Boys will reach this stage somewhat later . . . hopefully by twenty-three or so.

But for both genders, this is the time in childhood when a life-changing event occurs: going to school full-time. And there's another element a child is introduced to during these years. Although it's not nearly as important as school, it's one that often takes up as much of a child's time.

And that, of course, is organized sports.

When you were seven years old, even if you didn't play sports, it's likely that now, twenty-five years later, you claim that you did. In fact, you have probably convinced yourself that had you pursued the natural gifts God bestowed on you as a child, you would be playing with LeBron James instead of watching him. Or at least telling the guys at work that you watch him.

But whether you participated in youth sports or not, you need to be careful about exaggerating your past athletic accomplishments and prowess. This is especially true with your children, because they will actually believe what you tell them, and this could very well come back to bite you on the butt. And remember that this is the same butt that never moved off the bench during freshman volleyball, the only year you participated (sort of) in high school sports.

Picture this: One afternoon, you're dropping your seven-year-old off for his first preseason baseball practice when the president of the park league hurries up to your car. "Hey, Jim," he says to you, "we've got a problem. Big problem."

"Wow, Phil, what's up?"

"You know Jake Owens, the guy who was gonna coach your son's team this year?"

Of course you know him. He's thirty-eight, looks eighteen, and has the body of a Greek statue. Your wife says Jake Owens probably put the "J-O" in "J-O-C-K."

"Yeah, what about him?"

"Well," the president says, "he tore his Achilles in an Ironman last weekend. He's gone for the season, so I talked with the board, and we'd like you to take over the team."

"Me?" you ask, stunned.

"Yeah, your son tells me you played high school baseball. All-City, right?"

"Well, yeah . . ." you stammer. "But it was a very small city. Nothing more than a town, really. In fact, it should actually be called a 'burg.' That would be more accurate; I was All-Burg."

"I picked up the equipment at Jake's house. I'll get it out of my car for you." Apparently Phil is not a good listener.

"Jeez, I'd love to help out," you say, as sweat forms on your upper lip. "But I have a job."

"Not a real job. You're a writer," Phil says dismissively. "C'mon, Jim, the Orioles need you. And think of the excellent opportunity this would be to bond with your son."

"We're already pretty bonded," you answer as your temples start throbbing.

Phil sighs, disappointed. "OK, Jim, I understand. But if you don't do it, we may have to disband the team. Those twelve youngsters would certainly be disappointed."

You look over at the ragtag group, some of whom are chasing each other around the bases, while others throw their gloves at each other.

Ten minutes later, you and Phil are standing in front of a group of seven- and eight-year-olds sitting on the grass in front of you.

". . . And so, kids, it is my pleasure to introduce you to your new coach, Mr. Jim Granicki!"

The kids cheer, but none louder than your son, who looks up to you with the admiration he usually reserves for people like Derek Jeter or Lady Gaga.

That first day, you go the entire practice without taking the equipment out of the bag. Instead, you talk about things you know something about . . . teamwork, fair play, and the importance of the players eating all their vegetables. When you get home that night, your wife howls at the thought of you being a baseball coach. But she also gives you huge props for saving the day, and guarantees that the kids will love you.

Later, after your son goes to bed, you call three of your friends who actually do know a lot about baseball, and played a lot of it . . . one of them even in college. After hearing your plight, they all agree to come out and help.

When the season ends, the mighty Orioles finish with a record of eight wins and six losses. You didn't finish first, but you didn't finish last, either. And most importantly, the kids had a great time; you and your coaches never yelled at them and were nothing but encouraging. At the team party, every parent thanked you and your coaches for the time you put in and how positive you were with their children. Those parents with seven-year-olds asked if you'd be coaching next season, hoping their kids could be on your team again.

"Of course he's coaching next year," your son says proudly.

As you drive home from the party, you reflect on the season, and treasure what a wonderful experience it turned out to be. Not only was it fun, but thanks to your coaches, every player learned a lot about baseball.

But none as much as you.

★ ★ ★

Today, unlike generations past, sports are no longer the province of boys only. Thanks to some long overdue legislation by both the federal government and the NCAA, women's sports are now booming. From preschoolers to pros, from soccer to softball, females of all ages are now scoring goals, hitting home runs, sinking three-pointers, and draining twenty-five-foot putts, just like their male counterparts. And whereas young boys have had male sports stars to admire for decades, girls now have their own heroes to look up to in the form of Mia Hamm, Lisa Leslie, Jenny Finch, Lorena Ochoa, Danica Patrick, and hundreds of others.

And what does this mean for today's dads? It means that unlike dads of only two generations ago, you and your daughter can participate in activities that can involve *both* of you. Let's face it, twenty-five years ago, very few fathers and daughters were tossing the ball around in the front yard, or going to the driving range together, or playing one-on-one in the driveway. Well, today they are. Daughters and dads are participating in all sorts of sports together. And guess what, dads? As our daughters grow stronger and their talents are honed, we are getting worked!

Gone are the days when ballet, Girl Scouting, and gymnastics were a young girl's main extracurricular outlets—outlets that were usually the province of daughter and mother. Don't misunderstand; these are all very important activities and surely will continue to be. But they weren't exactly pursuits that a dad and his daughter could get together on. If you doubt this, have you ever heard a dad say, "Yankee–Red Sox game tonight? Gosh, I'd love to go, but I'm going to my daughter's Girl Scout meeting to teach them how to braid lanyards." Or, "Sorry, but I'm out for bowling tomorrow night; I have to work with my daughter on the closing section of *Swan Lake*."

Didn't think so.

Not only can sports bring dads and moms together with their kids, it can also be a valuable developmental tool for children. It can be a source of self-esteem that they're unable to realize elsewhere. It can teach the tenets of teamwork, fair play and the value of honest competition. And for a select few, it can offer a path to higher education that might otherwise be unavailable.

But for most children, it's just flat-out fun, as long as adults stay out of the way and let it be.

So if you're a dad who's got some free time and the right attitude, don't be afraid to volunteer to coach, even if you don't have any experience, or if you know nothing about the sport. The best thing is to be honest about it . . . unless, of course, you have three good friends who've really got game.

SEVEN

THE SEVEN-YEAR GLITCH

Congratulations; you are now the dad of a six-year-old. You survived teething, earaches, and first steps; you were able to jockey and jump through hoops to get her into a good preschool. And you were also able to obtain a second mortgage to pay for it all. But it was a wise decision, because your little girl has now moved on to the Bolt Academy's elementary school, where she is a proud first grader. You and your wife now consider yourselves a well-oiled and confident parenting team. Thanks to some diligent scheduling and duty splitting, you've also been able to maintain productive careers; but your combined goal is to salt away enough savings so your wife can leave the work force for good and have another child. Or two. You are well on your way toward that goal, and all is smooth sailing.

But then a weather front moves in.

One evening you're driving home from work with your daughter, Molly, in the seat next to you, just as she is after every school day. Your wife takes her to school each morning and you pick her up at 5:30 every evening, because Bolt offers after-school care until 6 PM. This is just another part of the parenting routine that you and your wife have down pat.

But when you pull into your driveway, you see your wife's car there. "That's odd," you think. She doesn't usually get home until after six.

"Mommy's home!" your daughter screams and runs into the house ahead of you.

"Hey, Jan," you say when you walk in. "You're home early. Everything OK?"

"Yeah, fine," she insists unconvincingly.

But you know better, because after more than seven years of marriage, you can tell when she's covering something up. You pull her aside and ask what's going on, but she whispers that it will have to wait until Molly goes to bed. You determine that if it can't be discussed in front of Molly, it must be serious.

Throughout dinner, you wonder what it could be. Did she get fired? Dang, and you were so close to meeting your financial goals! It has to be that; what else could it be? A divorce!? No way! Our marriage is terrific, you say to yourself. But then you recall her corporate Christmas party where you overheard her telling a co-worker, "Damn, that Xavier is a babe!" as she pointed to the twenty-eight-year-old French VP of international sales. And later, they danced the macarena together! That's it, you conclude. She's leaving me for a younger guy! You hate the French!

By the time Molly finally goes to bed at 8:30, your imagination has concocted a scenario in which your wife and Xavier are happily married and living in a château in the south of France. Of course, she got custody of Molly, who is overjoyed to have two newborn stepbrothers to go along with her younger dad. You, on the other hand, were devastated by the divorce; your work suffered, and you were soon terminated. You lost your house, your car, and even your pet, which snuck off with another dog. And to add insult to injury, it was a French poodle!

An hour later, your wife creeps out of Molly's room and quietly closes the door. You pounce on her in the hallway.

"It's about that Xavier, isn't it?" you say.

"Pardon?"

"That good-looking Frog," you say, spitting out the words.

"Ohmigod! How did you find out about it?" she asks, amazed.

"Oh, a man has his ways," you wail. "I suppose it's the talk of your office."

"No. No one knows," she says. "And I still can't believe that you do! Did I talk in my sleep?"

This is too much for you to take. You feel your knees start to weaken, so you lean against the wall for support.

"Do you really expect it to last?"

"Only for six weeks," she says. "But the money's worth it."

"Money? You're being paid?"

"Almost double what I make now."

"Oh, God!" You begin whimpering softly. "Just the thought of you two together . . ." You can't continue.

"Look, sweetie . . . Together? Who?"

"You and Frenchie."

"What are you talking about?"

"I'm talking about . . ." You stop when you see her strike her "I can't wait to hear this" pose; it's the one she uses whenever you jump to yet another boneheaded conclusion. "What are *you* talking about?" you say, turning things around on her.

"I'm talking about Xavier taking over our European operation. And me moving up into his job."

"That's it?" you say.

"That's it?" she says, hurt that you don't seem to be the least bit excited for her. "Isn't that enough?"

"Of course it is!" you shout with an excitement borne out of utter and total relief. "Congratulations, Mrs. Vice President," you say, lifting her off the floor and twirling her.

She shushes you not to wake Molly, and the two of you go into the den to talk about it. It's a great opportunity, she says, but she didn't want to say "yes" until she talked to you. The thing is, she has to attend a six-week orientation and corporate training course in New York, which is a two-hour plane ride from your home just outside Chicago. Even though she'll be home every weekend, from Friday afternoon until late Sunday evening, she didn't know if you could handle tending to Molly all by yourself during the week.

"Are you kidding?" you say, kissing her. "I'm her dad. Of course I can handle it."

Then, as you discuss some more of the logistics, you break open a bottle of wine to celebrate. A half hour later, you suggest that it might be time for bed.

"But it's only nine thirty," your wife says.

"True," you say. 'But I'm a little excited about this. I've never slept with a vice president before." (Not entirely true . . . but that was way before you met your wife. Besides, that young lady worked at a bank. *Everybody's* a vice president there.)

The following Sunday afternoon, you and your daughter are kissing and hugging your wife good-bye at the airport. Then, after she clears the security checkpoint, she calls back to you. "Remember, if you need any help, call Karen!"

"Karen, Schmaren," you call after her smugly. "Don't worry; Dad's got everything covered!"

When your wife disappears around a corner, you take Molly's hand securely in yours and the two of you head out of the terminal toward the parking structure. You're surprised—and a little peeved—that your wife felt she had to put your neighbor, Karen, on Stage One Red Alert in case goofy ole you couldn't handle things on your own. Of course you can handle it. You're the dad. You welcome the responsibility. Now, if you could just remember where you parked the car.

When you get home, you begin to pore through the volumes of instructions your wife left for you . . . just for the next five days. She also prepared five nights of meals, so you go into the fridge and pull out a glass Pyrex baking dish covered with Saran and marked "Sunday." Then you read her cooking instructions. "Preheat oven at 350 for 20 minutes, then bake for 35 minutes." The instructions go on to explain that there's a baguette in the freezer that you can defrost in the microwave, then slice, butter, and put in the broiler. There's also a bag of salad fixings in the crisper; just cut a tomato and you're good to go. So you turn the oven on, and exactly twenty minutes later you insert the lasagna.

While you wait, you and Molly set the table for two, and begin a game of Crazy Eights. About fifteen minutes later, you notice an odd smell coming from the oven; when you open it, you see that the Saran wrap sizzling as it melts all over the top of the lasagna. What happened? The instructions didn't say anything about removing the Saran first. You grab a wooden spoon and a potholder and try to scrape it off, but you make matters worse by blending the bubbling plastic into the sauce. Oh, great, you think. For your daughter's first meal with Dad, you'll be serving lasagna with melted petroleum products. And you haven't even gotten to the bread and salad yet.

You look to your daughter.

"Hey, Molls," you say.

"Yes, Daddy?"

"How do you feel about pizza?"

She smiles and gives you a confident thumbs-up.

Before her bedtime, you give Molly her bath and braid her hair, just like your wife showed you. She explained that if you wash Molly's hair at night and don't braid it, it will be a frizzy mess in the morning. After you finish your braiding job, you help Molly into her pajamas and tuck her in for the night.

"I love you, Daddy," she says as you kiss her.

"Love you too, Molly," you say.

You turn off the light and leave her room. As you walk down the hall, you pat yourself on the back. One night down and all is well. Then you remember to toss the lasagna; tomorrow is trash day and it's always a good idea to destroy the evidence.

The next morning, you get up early and shower, dress, and have some coffee before waking your daughter.

"Molly, honey," you whisper to the lump buried beneath her covers. "Time to get up."

She stirs, but then tries to go back to sleep. You sit on the side of her bed and jostle her gently. "C'mon, Molls, time for breakfast."

She grunts; she groans; she sleepily pulls the covers from over her head.

As she opens her sleepy eyes to see you staring down at her, your expression of shock must have given you away.

"Daddy, what's wrong?" she asks.

"Oh, nothing, honey," you lie. Then, on the pillow next to her, you spot the rubber bands that you thought you had so expertly applied to her braids. Her soft golden hair is flailing in every direction; it's as if she'd stuck her finger in a light socket.

You check your watch; there's still time to make things right, and you are a man who can react quickly to any emergency. You spring into action.

Less than forty-five minutes later, Molly is in the passenger seat of your car, dressed in her freshly pressed school uniform, with her hair in perfect braids.

Your cell phone rings. It's your wife; she's on a break from her seminar. She asks how everything is going so far.

"Perfect," you answer cheerily. "We're almost to school right now. Sure, she's right here."

You hand Molly your cell phone. "Mommy wants to talk to you."

"Hi, Mommy!" Molly chirps, excitedly. "Guess what? Last night we had pizza and this morning Auntie Karen came over and fixed my hair!"

You see the school approaching, so you grab the phone and employ a trick you learned from your dad. You bang your cell phone on the dashboard, and then put it to your ear. "Oops, sorry, honey," you say to your wife. "Must be out of range. Call you later."

You hang up as she was beginning to instruct you on how to drop off Molly at school. Jeez, you pick her up every afternoon . . . what does she think you are, an idiot?

Five minutes later, an angry car-pooling mom is honking her horn at you and yelling, "You idiot!"

"Can't you read the signs, nimrod?" screeches another. The sweat on your forehead is flowing freely as you read the sign that you pass by every afternoon, but have never paid much attention to: "ONE-WAY TRAFFIC! PICKUP LANE FROM 2:45 PM TO 6:00 PM. DROP-OFF LANE FROM 7:00 AM TO 8:10 AM."

Oops. As you try to back out, it seems that everyone in the traffic jam you have caused is honking at you, because you have broken the cardinal rule of car pooling: you have dropped off in the pickup lane!

When you pick up Molly after school, she hops in the car and hands you an envelope. Inside is a "traffic ticket" from the principal. Your penalty? For the spring school carnival, you are sentenced to one hour in the dunk tank.

But all things considered, with twenty-four hours under your belt, things could be worse.

And as the weeks pass, you get a better handle on your temporarily single dad duties, and your phone calls to your neighbor Karen drop to one every two days or so. The weekends with your wife home are always busy and fun-filled, and make you count the days until her training course comes to an end.

You figure that the worst is behind you. And you're essentially correct; but there is still one minor speed bump ahead. . . .

You've had a really sucky day at work. One of your big accounts is threatening to leave; your expense report got kicked back because of an exorbitant bill from a lunch with clients; and your computer's hard drive crashed. All you want to do is to go home, have dinner, put Molly to bed, have a really strong cocktail, and go to bed yourself. But you promised Molly and your absent wife you'd attend Back to School Night, so you arranged for Karen to pick up Molly from school and keep her until you get home.

As you drive to the school, traffic is horrible and you're yawning, so when you see a Starbucks ahead, you check your watch. You calculate that you've got just enough time for a quick stop and still make it on time. Nothing like a four-dollar cup of coffee to brighten your spirits.

When you walk in, you see you're in luck. The only person in front of you, a young female with earrings the size of hula hoops and a skirt of questionably short length, is already placing her order. Finally, something is going right today.

". . . venti macchiato with three shots," you hear her finish. Then, as you step forward to order, she pulls a list from the pocket of her beige jacket.

"And a grande mocha, nonfat, no whip, with only two pumps. A venti vanilla cappucino, dry." Let's see . . . Joanie wants a tall caramel frappucino with an extra shot; James wants a grande soy latte, no whip, no foam. And Laurie wants a . . ."

"Excuse me, miss," you say from behind.

She turns to you, "Yes, sir?" she says politely.

"Do you think I could jump in ahead of you? I'm in kind of a hurry."

"Oh, I only have one more," she says cheerily.

"I understand. But they'll have to make all of yours before they get to mine. And I really am pressed for time."

"Then, sir, you should have gone to McDonald's," she says with more politeness than you probably deserve. "But sure, Speed Racer, be my guest."

You nod your thanks, step in front of her and order a venti iced coffee.

The guy behind the counter says facetiously, "Yessir, right away!"

He fills a glass with ice, adds some coffee, and begins to put a lid on it.

"No need to do that," you say, "I'll add cream myself."

He hands you your coffee and you turn to head for the cream, not expecting the girl to be standing right behind you. You spill your iced coffee all over the front of her.

She screams as the ice goes down the inside of her blouse.

"Oh, God, I'm sorry," you say. Acting on impulse, you grab some napkins and begin dabbing her chest. Not a good move; she smacks your hand.

"What is wrong with you?" she demands.

"I'm sorry; I didn't mean anything by that. I'm a married man."

"Poor woman," the girl says.

"Look, I'm really sorry. Honest. But I have to go." You take out your money clip and hand her two twenties. "Let me pay for your coffee. And to get your blouse cleaned. I am so sorry!"

And then you get the hell out of there. You drive like a madman, sipping what little is left of your iced coffee. Can this day get any worse?

You make it to Molly's school a few minutes ahead of time. You find the first grade classroom and look around at the students' drawings and penmanship papers hanging on the walls. You can't help feeling proud that Molly has more than her share of papers displayed, all with gold stars. You also notice the framed diploma from the Loyola University Chicago School of Education. The diploma's recipient is Marissa Carlyle, who you know is Molly's teacher. Very impressive; it's nice to see that your tuition is paying for quality people. You spot an empty desk toward the back of the room, and as you attempt to squeeze yourself into it, you hear: "Hello, parents. I'm Miss Carlyle; sorry for being a few minutes late, but I had a little accident."

When you hear her voice, you freeze. It can't be, can it? You don't want to look up, but you must. Sure enough, there's the girl from Starbucks; she's still wearing the short skirt and earrings, but over her blouse is a bulky Bolt

Academy sweatshirt. As she scans all the parents, she spots you. So you do the only thing you can.

"I'm sorry," you say, "but I'm in the wrong room. My daughter, I mean my son, is in third grade."

And, in a final moment of embarrassment, when you stand, the undersized desk stands with you. So you leave the room, desk still attached.

You finally free yourself and run to your car. You hurry home, pick up Molly from Karen's, and put her to bed. Then, with all finally quiet, you have that cocktail you've been wanting. Then you have another.

The rest of your single dad experience goes without any major incidents. But when your wife's training course is over and she returns home, you vow to never again let her out of your sight for more than twenty-four hours.

Then, five months later, you receive a cold reminder that there is, indeed, still a trace of justice remaining in today's world. At the school's spring carnival, the first person to dunk you is Miss Carlyle.

She is also the second. And the third.

Turns out, the young lady has a hell of an arm.

EIGHT

LET'S DO IT AGAIN

Like the dads you've read about so far—and most dads everywhere—you probably remember every detail of the day you learned that you were going to be a father for the first time.

It might have been over a romantic dinner; it might have been via an excited phone call at work; or it might have been a visit from the really steamed father of your girlfriend.

But whatever the circumstances—good or bad—they are likely etched in your memory. Now, let us ask you a question; and please be honest: Where were you when you found out that your wife was pregnant with your second, or third, or . . .

Don't get us wrong. It's not that you didn't talk about expanding your family, because you did, and both of you were ready and willing. But instead of getting the news over a romantic dinner, it's just as likely that it took place in a fast-food drive-through.

Imagine that you and your wife are in line, waiting to order. You picked up your three-year-old daughter from day care and went directly to the video store, where you searched for anything that she hadn't seen yet, as long as it featured either a singing starfish or a beautiful princess who's in love with an ugly guy. You and your wife have each had a hard week at work, and all you want to do is get your food, get home, eat, and relax.

"Welcome to Burger and Sushi World," says the teenager over the speaker. "What can I get you?"

"I'll have the yellowfin tuna burger with everything. And an order of chili cheese fries." Then you turn to your wife. "What about you, honey?"

"I'm not hungry," she says with a queasy look on her face.

"Touch of the flu?" you ask.

"Nah," she says. "I think I'm pregnant."

"Wow, all right!" you say as you kiss her. Then you turn to your daughter in the back seat. "What do you want, Sarah?"

And there you have it.

Having your first child is not unlike your first trip to a place like Disneyland. It's magical; you remember every detail of the experience.

Yes, if you take a second trip to Disneyland it will still be wonderful and exciting; but it will lack the newness and freshness of the first. Then, if you happen to take a third, fourth, and fifth trip, it becomes more familiar to you each time. Then, if you go a sixth time, it's "OK, dude, it's a small world. I get it already!"

Particularly in dads, this tendency to be somewhat blasé about non-firstborns can begin with your wife's pregnancy and continue until the non-firstborn child reaches his early teens and finally says to his older sibling, "How come Mom and Dad like you best?"

For example, all those birthing classes you dutifully attended to prepare for your first child? For your second child, it's "Fuggedaboutit!" Really, what is there to learn that you don't already know? Has breathing changed in the last three years? Relaxing? The only difference might be that your wife learned some endearing new curse words to hurl at you during delivery.

But that likely won't matter, because your wife—having previously experienced the beauty of natural childbirth—will now have at least one anesthesiologist on her speed dial. For a mom to repeat natural childbirth for the sheer joy of it would be like you repeating your vasectomy for the same reason.

Also, during the second pregnancy, you will have a lot more time—and a lot more money—than you did during the first; no need to buy a crib, mobile, bassinette, playpen, or clothes—you already have all that stuff. So you come to see the arrival of your second-born as more than gaining another beautiful child; you see it as reclaiming your garage as well.

For those of you who doubt any of this, here's a little test for you: On your second-born's first birthday, check your photo album to see how many pictures you have of him during his first year. Two hundred? Two fifty? Not so bad. Now check the photos of your firstborn; more albums than The Stones, right? You have two hundred pictures of his baptism alone; a hundred and fifty more of the big family gathering afterwards. But when your second-born was baptized, it was only you, the godparents, and the priest. And instead of having a party afterwards, you hurried to the park, where your older child had a soccer game.

And finally, here's a scenario that has played out in thousands of homes across America with more than one child. . . .

When your cute firstborn was about eighteen months old, the two of you played a game in your backyard where he would run at you and you would gently "tackle" him, and he would laugh uncontrollably. But one day when you gently took him down, he hit the ground and immediately began screaming bloody murder. When you picked him up to see what was wrong, you discovered that when you tackled him, he smacked his cute little head on a lawn sprinkler. "Aaaaaagggggghhh!" he wailed. You checked the back of his head and saw that he already had a goose egg the size of a small ball bearing.

God! What had you done to your precious baby?

And that's exactly what your wife yelled as she flew out the back door and ran to you. When you explained, she took the sobbing infant into her arms. "I told you that you play too rough with him," she said.

"Gee, honey," you say, "thanks for trying to make me feel better."

Then she touches the baby's head. "This bump's the size of a golf ball!" And then, as she parts his hair to get a better look, she exclaims, "And I think it's bleeding, too!" You jump to your feet to take a look. Yep, there's blood, all right. Only a drop or two, but for a baby that size, you reason that a drop could equal at least a quart or two of yours. While your wife tries to soothe her baby, you race into the house, all the while wondering if your son will ever be able to forgive you. You suspect not, and picture him at his high school graduation, where he's the valedictorian: "I'd like to thank my mom for all that she's done for me, especially saving me from my dad, who tried to kill me in our backyard!"

You call the pediatrician, forgetting that it's Saturday. You get his office answering machine and leave a frantic message, using phrases like "bump the size of a volleyball," and "bleeding horribly." He calls you back in ten minutes from his country club, where he's playing golf with his wife. After the doctor calms you down and gets the real facts, he says that it's probably a harmless bump; babies' skulls are made to weather such things. He tells you if the situation worsens to call him back. Then he hangs up. You can't believe his nonchalance. Your formerly high opinion of him takes a nosedive. And what's more, you ask yourself, "What kind of guy plays golf with his wife?"

Twenty minutes later, you and your wife burst into the emergency room, carrying your baby, who has stopped crying and is now seemingly quite happy wolfing down a box of animal crackers. You suspect that this sudden spike in appetite is due to his blood loss.

You check in with a triage nurse, who takes the baby's vital signs. Blood pressure, pulse, and heart rate are all normal. There is no clamminess, and his pupils look normal. She then tells you to take a seat; a physician will be with you as soon as possible.

Two hours later, you are still sitting there. Your baby has fallen asleep, and three patients who came in after you have already been seen by a doctor: an older man with severe chest pains, a pregnant woman who was starting contractions three weeks early, and a guy who fractured both arms trying to dive off his roof into his pool. You didn't mind the first two taking priority, but your precious eighteen-month-old having to wait for a lunatic? But before you can complain, you're called in to see a physician.

She checks out his eye motion, his reflexes, and tries to locate what you call the "huge gash" on his head. Everything checks out perfectly normal: he's fine. Your son has apparently forgotten all about the accident and is now only interested in trying to break a tongue depressor in two. You get home around 7:30 PM and reward your little man for his amazing bravery with ice cream and cookies.

Whew, that was a close call.

Now, it's four years later and you're playing the same tackling game in the backyard with your second-born child. You tackle him near the same sprinkler.

Thwack!

As he howls, you pick him up and start toward the house. You probe his head and feel the bump forming. There's a little more blood than last time.

"Honey, could you get some ice," you casually call in to your wife. "Jared banged his head on a sprinkler." Then you take your wailing child into the family room. "It's OK, Jared. Mommy's getting some ice for your boo-boo." Then you put him on your lap and switch on the television.

"Hey, look, buddy. Notre Dame–Penn State. Sweet!" And as you bounce him on your knee, his crying subsides.

And another crisis solved by an experienced dad.

NINE

ANGELS TO DEMONS: THE TWEEN AND TEEN YEARS

Much to your delight, the ages from age seven through eleven seemed rather tranquil in terms of dad-dom, probably because there was not much spare time for anything drastic to happen. You and your wife spent all your free time schlepping to school, soccer, baseball, and band practice. For children, these years are like an extended spring training: they take things at a slow pace, learning new techniques and tricks while getting their bodies in shape for the real thing, which is lurking just around the corner.

And although your kids have grown in height during these ages, they are still little people . . . just with longer pants. If you have a son, you will notice a change in his voice, which is now in that grating range where it can't decide whether it belongs to Luciano Pavarotti or Roseanne. If you have a daughter, it is likely that she has taken to wearing a training bra. You think that's cute, but exactly what it is that she's training remains a mystery to you.

So you've survived eleven years and you're feeling pretty good about things. You are now fully invested in your "Inner-Dadness" and have now turned your attention to transforming your children into conscientious, contributing citizens who will make the world a better place. Who will

leave negligible carbon footprints. Who will be able to read the "Apartments for Rent" ads before they're thirty-two. You try to stay on top of your children's schoolwork, which has taught you that to a great extent, no, you are *not* smarter than a fifth grader. Your children's homework becomes, naturally, more complicated the older they get, and you've wisely opted not to make matters worse by "helping" with it, especially after your past efforts have earned several quiz scores of D, with the odd C-. The teacher's comments on those papers seemed particularly unfair and immature, especially in regard to your take on biology and history. You were never really any good at math, so you stayed out of that one, perhaps explaining your child's B+ in pre-algebra.

But still, you are cruising along, displaying your dad "A" game. But then one day something happens. And it happens at the very moment you say to your child, "Happy twelfth birthday!"

It's around this time that everything changes . . . and it's not just *your* children; it's their friends, too. Is it just your imagination, or do they now seem to have a bit of an edge about them? They all used to be such angels! But there are suddenly some pretty clear indications that "the times, they are a-changin'." Tribal markings that make *Lord of the Flies* look tame begin to appear. Black fingernail polish and magenta hair are seemingly everywhere.

Kids seem to have a need to self-identify as trouble-makers, just like you used to see yourself as a "bad boy," remember? And if you haven't figured that out by their behavior, they are happy to provide you with unassailable proof in the form of goth makeup or a predilection for showing off their underwear. Skateboards appear, and you find yourself toying with the implications of selling your "tween" for medical experiments.

There is a reason why, up until now, your life with your child has been all love and light, puppy dogs and smiles and hugs, baby smells and terrycloth jammies, and in general, joy to the world. Because if dads first experienced twelve years like the next four or five that are to follow, they would have jumped off Darwin's *Beagle* and allowed the world to pass to its most durable and populous heirs—the cockroaches.

Welcome to the middle years, the years from approximately ages twelve through sixteen, during which your child begins to make the grueling transition from cute cuddly child to irascible know-it-all teenager. This can be a difficult ride, and for all involved, it is anything but boring.

TEN

MALCONTENT IN THE MIDDLE

Your introduction to middle school is a true baptism by fire! You may live close enough to your school for your tweener to shuffle there. But no matter what, at some point you will find yourself driving to that institution to drop off, pick up, or bail out your child. Our first bit of advice is that a mature dad absolutely *must* resist the temptation to pull his car over and randomly start trying to smack that sullen look off the face of every kid in the vicinity. When you pull up to the crosswalk, whether there's a traffic light or a crossing guard involved or not, just be aware that no; the kids smirking at you while dragging themselves across the street cannot possibly walk any slower, otherwise they would be walking slower. That look of insouciance and their joy at making you wait for them is born of the absolute certainty that—should you foolishly get out of your car to do something about it—they could evade you in a footrace. And the aggravating part about it is that they could. Even with backpacks large enough to hitchhike across Europe— if they could look at a map and *find* Europe—these kids are almost at the height of their physical prowess while you— let's be kind here—are probably not. The only time older guys in suits run down younger, more agile prey is on TV cop shows. And those guys have guns.

You will also notice a disconnect here that seems to be gender biased. Those of you with sons will notice that his priorities now generally involve his skateboard, his video console, and scratching himself. He seems to be taking a lot of showers now, even though he hasn't taken one in PE all year. Grades are way down the list, right above caring about what you think. It is from this point on that you are eternally grateful that you didn't start your own business just so you could leave it to him.

Girls, on the other hand, often still perform well in school. But their lives outside of class are fraught with drama. Observe any group of girls this age and you'll notice that their universal language is the hug. They hug before class, after class, and between classes. They hug if they've seen you or if they haven't seen you. And they often hug people they don't even know. They definitely hug any boy bold enough to be in their presence. Dads are prone to give their daughters a lot of leeway during this stage, mostly because of our general ignorance about all females and our primal fear of the mystery of menstruation.

Meanwhile, we usually just dismiss our sons as upstart punks, forgetting that the hormonal changes they're going through can be more confusing than a Yoko Ono album. The only thing these two groups—teenage sons and teenage daughters—share is an ability to roll their eyes so far back in their head that it's possible they're looking at their brain. Or *for* it. You'll learn to expect this response whenever you're in close proximity to a teenager. Or whenever you voice your agreement with one by saying, "I am so down with that!"

You'll go to Back to School Nights less frequently; but on your rare appearances, you'll observe that teachers of middle school seem to be a breed apart. They are the kind of people who bungee jump. Most of their cars are equipped with ski racks, and they all have very nice teeth. They are high on adrenalin and they will do anything—even stand in front of a class full of malevolent seventh graders—to get their rush. They are generally free spirits who are closer in temperament to their students than they are to corporate chieftains. The female teachers are not afraid to dress like Stevie Nicks or to play the Gipsy Kings in class. The male teachers will actually horse around with their students on the playground, or explain that the kids need to learn their latest bizarre lesson in social studies in case they ever appear on *Jeopardy!*. If, as they say, there is a special place in heaven for teachers, you hope the special place for these people is not anywhere near where you are.

During these challenging years, you will receive truck-loads of ridiculous and unusable advice on how to deal with the aliens who have taken over the bodies of your beautiful children. Here's some more from us:

Remove their bedroom doors. As a responsible parent, you don't want any kind of covert or subversive activities taking place right under your own nose. If Saddam Hussein had grown up in a bedroom without a door, he might have won the Nobel Peace Prize. Or at least learned how to trim a moustache.

But if you choose to leave the door on because his room is near the living quarters of the regular members of the family, it would be wise to install a lock on the outside. The very *last* thing you want to be doing is peering regularly into the trash heap in your kid's room that only a forensic anthropologist might make sense out of.

Do not—and this can't be emphasized strongly enough—*do not ever* pick up socks in your adolescent son's room. In fact, laundry in general should be avoided unless you are employing a pair of tongs and wearing a biohazard suit. In a related bit of advice, let him take as many showers as he wants. In fact, encourage them.

Do try to encourage as many extracurricular activities as you can. If your child has any kind of athletic ability at all, this is an easy sell. If music is their thing, it's OK to encourage their inner Jonas Brother or Hannah Montana. Never forget that there's an alarming number of death metal and gangsta rap groups out there. Would you rather spend a few years staring at a poster of Miley Cyrus or at the Insane Clown Posse?

Also, you may need to totally rethink your "grounding" strategy of sending your misbehaving child to their room. Go and take a look at that room. Does it bear a striking resemblance to Strategic Air Command headquarters? Between computers, scanners, iPods, cell phones, TVs, DVD players, and what could very well be facilities for conducting cold fusion experiments or yellowcake uranium research, there is hardly any activity that can't be duplicated or even improved upon in your child's inner sanctum. While you thought your son was being punished, he's teeing off on the sixth hole at Pebble Beach while catching up on Jenna Jameson's latest release! (You can sneak in and get her Web site when he's in the shower. You're welcome.) The only way you will get your child's attention is by confiscating all power cords and batteries. Now when you threaten, "You can just go to your room and think about what you've done," there is a remote possibility that your child may be forced to do just that.

As long as you also took the remote.

ELEVEN

THE HIGH SCHOOL YEARS

The middle school years seemed to fly by. You've watched your child stumble toward physical, if not emotional, maturity. If you have a daughter, this is when your wife will take her to buy a *real* bra. If you have a son, this is about when he will finally decide to ditch his Spider-Man pajamas. In just three short years, your child has gone from a scrawny, scared seventh grader to a confident, top-of-the-heap ninth grader.

That's a shame, because here comes the high school smackdown, where your child will once again be at the lowest rung of the confidence ladder, a piece of discarded spearmint gum stuck to the sole of some senior's flip-flop.

But as a dad, you are entering the home stretch, depending, of course, on how many times after your first child was born you've had to mutter, "What? Again?" when the birth of another child was announced. You haven't had to use a babysitter in years, which means you've forgotten just what it was like to have a strange teenager in your house while you were out, rummaging through your personal stuff, breaking almost everything she touched, and then demanding ten dollars an hour for the privilege of having her there.

Your problem now is that you will soon have *many* teen-agers lurking around your house, all of them strange, and each one dropping opinions, odors, and annoying observations while emptying your refrigerator and trying your patience. You will only have to pay one of them though—the one that lives with you.

As your teen enters high school, you would do well to abandon the "when I was your age" technique of teaching by parables. To your children, you went to high school long ago in a galaxy far, far away. The way they see it, you were probably as clueless then as you are now. They don't care if you were varsity everything, or even a rock star in the chess club, because now you have the title "Mr." in front of your name. And Mr., as any teenager knows, stands for "Dweeb."

But, of course, you were Joe Cool back then, right? This means you never experienced the high school rite of initiation that still exists today: freshmen getting stuffed into their lockers by upperclassmen. No way. You saw it as a humiliating practice; but now, as a dad, you begin to see that it might have some value, as you imagine what it would be like if you had lockers in your home. Now how many times in a twenty-four-hour period do you think you'd be tempted to grab your wisenheimer high school freshman by the shirt collar and shove him inside, slamming and locking the door behind him?

But you need to be mature as well as sympathetic to the intimidation factor involved in being a first-year high schooler. Your fourteen-year-old, who only two weeks ago spent a weekend with friends playing army, is now sharing hallways with burly eighteen-year-olds who will soon be joining the army. You remember that when you were a high school freshman, you felt very alone and out of place the first few months. Especially crammed into that cold, dark locker. So, experienced dad that you are, you know

that this is a time in which adolescents yearn for accep-
tance. That is why you suggest to your child, who is not an
athlete, that he join one of the hundreds of campus clubs
or organizations available to him. Surprisingly enough, he
takes your advice; and soon, you find yourself finagled into
becoming a member of the Parcheesi Club Boosters. And
when they hold their fund-raising car wash, one warm,
sunny Saturday in late September, you feel it is your duty to
support it. After all, where else can you pay $15 for a wash
that leaves your car looking worse than when you started?

So you hop in your company-issued Ford Taurus and
set off for the car wash. As you get close, you see several
girls—mature girls; young women, actually—cavorting in
bikinis. Are these exhibitionist older sisters of some of the
students? Possibly even young moms? You know that this
kind of racy come on is meant to appeal to any one of
several base male instincts, but you decide to concentrate
on one that doesn't involve the Mann Act.

When you pull in, you are directed to an area where
you will fork over your money to a hyper-organized mom
with a severe haircut and $150 running shoes. You are glad
she left her bikini at home. She's leaning on the fender of
her Land Rover and barely takes her eyes off her iPhone,
and although you expect change, she assumes that you—a
booster just like her—don't need it, since small bills are
really more of an inconvenience than anything else. So she
stuffs all of your money into a Cuban cigar box and directs
you further down the line, where you see more young ladies
in bathing suits and others in T-shirts.

Wet T-shirts.

Then you notice that these T-shirts have the name of
your son's high school stenciled on the front, along with
"Parcheesi Club Member."

Member? These girls are high school students? How could that be? Were they held back a year? Or two? Or three?

As you pull into the washing area, you look ahead and spot your son. He is currently manning the hose and is happily squirting these women-children with cold water, and his punishment seems to be a friendly pelting with soapy sponges. You look at him, then at the young ladies and begin to put two and two . . . and then two more together. Now you understand why he chose the Parcheesi Club. All right! Your boy is not as goofy as he seems.

Then you are distracted when one of the girls leans over and begins soaping your windshield.

Careful of what you're staring at there, Mr. Polanski—there are laws against what you're thinking in most states. So you pick up the sports page you brought with you and read the scores from last night's games.

Good call.

Later, you are at a *real* car wash where they're trying to remedy the streaks and smears inflicted on your car by your parcheesi-playing pals.

Your car looks a lot better.

But as the paunchy guy sprays your windshield, you have to admit that he does lack a certain pizzazz.

TWELVE

DRIVING MISS (OR MISTER) CRAZY

You thought this day would never come! The same kid who uses the trampoline to jump over the cactus in the backyard; the same one who put the sand crabs into his swim trunks just to see what they felt like; the very same knucklehead who piloted his skateboard down the handrail of eight flights of stairs at the park and successfully completed five of them before the unfortunate mishap that may render him childless for the rest of his life, is about to get a learner's permit!

No longer will watching you daughter accelerate her Barbie Big Wheel down the driveway into traffic be your biggest concern. She will now be at the helm of two tons of metal capable of moving about three times as fast as she thinks it can. Do not waste any time here—call the insurance company immediately!

First, a word of caution: There's a very good reason why driver's training programs exist. It's been found that the trauma associated with parents choking off the windpipe of their teenage driving student has a deleterious effect on the learning curve. And the likelihood of you, as a dad, experiencing a grand mal seizure, a fatal spike in blood pressure, or the kind of cheap scare associated with slasher movies while attempting to tutor your young driver is extremely high. You were probably the kind of dad who enjoyed

taking your child out on her first bike, starting off with training wheels and—just like all of us—running along beside her until she magically discovered the solution to the mystery of balance. You may also have been the kind of hands-on parent who decided to teach your child how to ski or snowboard. He was timid. He faltered. But eventually, after falling under every possible circumstance and crashing into every available obstacle, his perseverance paid off and now he schusses circles around you.

When you peer out across the dashboard of the family van, wishing it had a set of dual controls, you can only focus on the oncoming SL600 that is making a left turn right across your path, its driver blissfully unaware of the imminent danger he's put himself into. Your student goes to his default position—honking the horn and shouting whatever Anglo-Saxon words you regrettably uttered in front of him when you were behind the wheel in the same type of situation. But there'll be plenty of time for recriminations later. From the shotgun seat, you stomp on your brakes, only to realize that you've put a depression in the floorboard while your car continues to hurtle towards an epic deductible. Finally, with a squeal of tires, you come to a halt. You have a small sense of satisfaction that the inertia reel on your seatbelt performed flawlessly, and you're thankful that your air bags didn't deploy.

With that characteristic strain in your voice that your teenager knows so well, you attempt a modulated request to change places while trying to control your breathing. Your teen is probably so scared that he can't even muster up an insult! This means that it's definitely time for you to consider the Busy Bee Driving Academy to help you keep your sanity and your bodywork intact.

With the help of a total stranger who displays the kind of cavalier attitude accessible only to people who are driving someone else's car, your child eventually passes her driving test. You are no longer an on call twenty-four-hour taxi service, and your new life of freedom and bliss nearly dazzles you with promise. But your euphoria is dampened when small scrapes and dents begin appearing on the car.

"Do you know anything about that?" you ask your teenage daughter as you point to a hole in the rear of your car where your left taillight used to be.

There's a 50/50 chance that she will become confrontational and say, "Jeez, Dad, why are always blaming me for everything?"

You explain that when you drove the car home from work yesterday, the taillight was right where you left it. And she was the only person to drive the car since.

"Did you ever think that maybe someone backed into me at the party last night?" she asks in a tone that says she thinks you are a true dunderhead.

"Party? I thought you were at Lisa's, working on your science project." Way to go, dunderhead; you've got her cold. No way she can squirm out of this one.

But in an amazing twist of logic that can only come from the mouth of a teenage daughter—or a philandering politician—she says, "Thanks a lot! You don't trust me about anything, do you?"

And then she storms out.

But if she's smart, when you point out the missing taillight, she'll look at you and her bottom lip will begin to quiver. "Oh, Daddy, I'm sorry," she'll say as she starts to cry. "I backed into a tree coming out of Lisa's house after we worked on our science project." Then she takes the tears up a notch or two. "I am such a loser! I can't drive! My grades suck! I'm going to my sophomore formal with my cousin! I don't know why you and Mom let me live here!"

You take her in your arms and console her. "There, there, honey; it's only a taillight."

Nice going, Dad. You ought to change your name to "Guitar Hero," 'cause, you just got played!

With a newly minted Dale Earnhardt, Jr., or Danica Patrick in the house, you will learn to fully explore the capacity and endurance of your fuel tank as never before, often wondering if you have enough gas to make it to the end of the driveway, much less the corner gas station. And in case you doubted it, yes—the family van or station wagon can burn rubber, and you've got the bald tires to prove it.

The fact is, today's intrepid young drivers are faced with far more distractions than we were. Video games have convinced your teen that not only is he capable of turning in NASCAR-caliber lap times around town, but that he or she can also text, tweet, knock back an energy drink, snap a photo of the hottie in the next car, and sing along to his or her iPod all at the same time. There is a pretty obvious message here: Never allow a teen behind the wheel of a car, especially a car that you own or even remotely care about. Driving should be restricted to people between the ages of twenty and seventy. Before twenty, people lack the maturity to drive; after seventy, they can rarely see over the steering wheel. But the law says that teens are allowed to drive at some point, so you'll just have to learn to trust them. Hang in there and gut it out. Your reward might very well be your teen growing into a responsible adult who will pick you up from "the home" and drive you to find some soft ice cream and a box of adult diapers.

In fact, you might still have some diapers left over from that first driving lesson.

THIRTEEN

CLASS ACTION

In between the athletic events and pep rallies, the school plays and the art shows, the academic decathlons and the band concerts, the endless bake sales and Monte Carlo nights, fashion shows and other fund-raisers, you're amazed that educators have somehow managed to shoehorn genuine academic classes into the average high school curriculum.

Of course, it's very unlikely that your teen will ever have anything positive to say about these classes, because he or she considers them obtuse and overrated. This is because these classes deal with things like language, history, and math. To hear your Rhodes Scholar talk, you'd think that the classroom is nothing more than a delivery system for humiliation and a constant stream of unjust and unwarranted teacher criticism and discipline. In the ninth and tenth grades, this may not be far from the truth, except for the unjust and unwarranted part. High school classes are roughly equivalent to a cage match, and only the most ferocious teachers are capable of taming their opponents in the desks.

At this stage of their academic development, high school freshmen and sophomores see classes as nothing more than a venue to showcase their latest hip gear. These are the formative years when a substantial percentage of kids learn the importance of style over substance, of image over depth.

97

And many of these students will carry this knowledge with them as they move on to lucrative careers as fashion models or mortgage brokers. And as you see this academic ennui grow in your child, the first two years of high school can be a troubling time for you as well. You throttle back on all those grandiose dreams of a scholarship to an Ivy League school and begin to focus more on things like the penal code and the short list of occupations where literacy is not a requirement. Perhaps a career as a hit man. Or a television executive.

But then come junior and senior years, when panic sets in for any child who even vaguely entertained the option of college. Even for those students who are not really driven by a thirst for knowledge, and who hold the antics of Harold and Kumar, Will Ferrell, and Borat as their intellectual benchmarks, attending college can be the holy grail of stalling off the inevitable annoyance of real life until a more convenient time, usually described as "later." Like the grasshopper in the fable, your teen will hopefully realize that he or she has fiddled away two years while the steadfast ants in the honors classes are sitting pretty on fat GPAs and looking forward to achieving formidable SAT scores.

Your child's apprehension, along with yours, will start to morph into anxiety after a spin through "College Night," where carefully chosen counselors from schools around the country advise your student on the enormous opportunities available at their respective school. These educators tout their school's graduation rate, endowments, and number of Nobel Prize winners. Your child, however, tries to bring the conversation around to essentials like cheap snowboarding passes, beer pong competitions, the availability of hot chicks/hot guys, and the closest, most bodacious venues for spring break.

As your child's anxiety about getting into college blossoms into full-blown fear, you will see a significant change in study habits, in that there will actually be some. And if your child's grades shoot up to a level where college may in fact be an option, you will more than likely be prodded into taking a "road trip" during junior year to check out the possibilities. The scope and expense of this trip usually depends on your teen's cumulative GPA. If it's 4.2 to 3.8, those airline tickets to Harvard and Stanford can be costly, although with grades that good, a scholarship is certainly possible. A GPA of 3.7 to 3.0 may require extensive air travel as well, especially if your child can throw a football over the Great Wall of China, or if he or she played first viola in the high school chamber orchestra. GPAs below 3.0 will normally involve nothing more than a lengthy drive around your state, or a trip to any college on an island.

Regardless of your destination, these scouting trips usually take place somewhere around the spring recess. (Note to college recruiters: if your institution has lagging attendance, there is no more powerful recruiting tool on campus than the halter top or tight bicycle shorts, particularly if you're knee-deep in snow.) Students lounging on the quad, throwing Frisbees or playing guitars, can get the attention of the most uninterested prospect. There is another segment of applicants to whom the off-campus fraternity or sorority house, complete with real-life action figures drinking beer before noon, might be the deciding factor. Although this is certainly not the best criterion to use when choosing a college, there could be an upside if your student leans in this direction, as it is likely to result in a college experience that is short and inexpensive.

As a mature and responsible dad, you need to be a realist and temper your expectations, and to not put subliminal pressure on your child by softly humming the Notre Dame fight song during dinner. Trust us, if your child doesn't tell you directly, his or her body language will let you know when each rejection letter arrives. And while common sense suggests that there should be no charge for receiving a letter that begins with, "No way, José," each and every college your child applies to wants close to $100 for that privilege. It's up to you to decide how many times you want to roll the dice, and which schools are worth the effort. Even if accepted, would your student make a go of it at Death Valley Junior College?

In the first couple of months of senior year, students go through the time-honored tradition of firing off applications to the schools were they hope to spend the next four, five, or six years. At this point, they are cautioned by teachers at school not to slack off on their academics—most colleges expect the same high standard of effort from your child right until they are humping their inflatable furniture up the stairs to the dorm room. Your student, like most others, will grudgingly take this to mean that he must put in his time at high school through the holidays, but not much longer.

Unless your child has somehow managed to flimflam a college into an early decision, he or she will most likely be anguishing over the application process right up through January. Then they can continue with the time-honored ritual of developing facial tics and heart palpitations, frantically tearing through the mailbox two and three times a day, and generally throwing up on a regular basis until the responses start to arrive in April. In some instances, this will not be an end to this behavior. It's possible that you yourself will get caught up in this mania, particularly after sweatshirts from colleges around the country begin to appear on other kids at the high school.

It's even worse when dads of these students begin sporting those sweatshirts as well. You hope your child gets accepted soon, because you want to wear one, too! There's one particular institution you favor, and in your mind, you picture yourself rooting for this college's football team in the fall, or wryly observing that their English department has a number of Pulitzers to the faculty's credit, or even defending the most recent campus demonstration because it was for a wonderful humanitarian cause. But you need to keep your emotions in check. Students are already going through enough torment to render them clinically depressed. No sense in raising the bar yet again while they're still on their way down the track with pole in hand, ready for the plant and the vault.

The smartest thing you can do at this time is to let them know that you'll always be there for them, regardless whether they're accepted or rejected. But just in case, you might want to lose a few pounds so you'll look good in that sweatshirt.

FOURTEEN

DANCES WITH WOLVES

But even as close as your daughter puts her nose to the grindstone, how much she worries about getting into college, finding a job, or how your son is going to convince you to support him for the next couple of years until he signs a record deal, nothing will interfere with the signal event in the life of any high schooler worth his iPod play-list. That event, of course, is the prom.

The high school prom serves, for many, as the ultimate achievement, not only in their high school careers, but, regrettably, in their entire lives. You saw them at your recent high school reunion—the athlete or the beauty queen, the rocker or the science expo finalist—who just can't seem to get past that watershed night. They've put on weight now. They've just gone through another divorce. They're still living in their parents' basement. They may even be mowing your lawn. Whether it's because of the attendant hoopla that surrounds the prom or because of the dismal circumstances of their current life is unimportant.

And now, as you're helping your son learn the vagaries of the cummerbund, or watching your wife help your daughter with the bow on the back of her seven-million-dollar dress, you cannot believe that you are old enough to be the dad of a prom-goer.

You feel a certain amount of fatherly pride that your child might just have the makings of what could be a relatively responsible and productive adult. As you and your wife wait for your son to emerge from his bedroom in his tux, you know that this is a big night for him, and you hope it's full of fun and a source of wonderful memories for him, just as yours was for you . . . especially memories of Irene Castagnola.

"What are you smiling at?" your wife asks.

"Oh, nothing," you say. "Just hard to believe that we're old enough to have a kid old enough to go to prom."

As she smiles, you remember how beautiful Irene looked that night. You and she had been dating nearly six months, and although you really liked each other, you were fumbling, nervous, and inexperienced teenagers whose amorous experimentation was limited to very passionate kissing and occasional, tentative rubbing. You were, like many of your friends, stumbling toward adulthood, and you were trying to get there as fast as your legs—or other parts of your body—could carry you. You can't recall much of the prom itself, other than the allure of Irene's perfume when you danced close. But it would be hard to forget what happened after the prom, when you and Irene . . .

"How do I look?" your son asks, exploding from his room in a tux that appears to be a tribute to Don "Magic" Juan, the Bishop of Pimps. Although a black tuxedo with scarlet lapels and a royal blue ruffled shirt might be appropriate if one is a maitre d' at an ethnic restaurant, you think he looks pretty goofy. But your wife made you promise not to say anything.

So you don't. But you made no promise about laughing.

"What, Dad?" your son asks.

"Oh, nothing," you answer as your wife scowls at you. "I was just thinking about my prom. I wore black tuxedo pants and a white dinner jacket." This reminds you of how quickly you ripped off that dinner jacket when you and Irene . . .

Your doorbell rings; it's your son's pal, Eric. They're double dating, and Eric's driving what will undoubtedly be the coolest vehicle ever to hit the prom scene: a camouflaged Bradley fighting vehicle limo that his dad scored for only three hundred bucks for the night . . . ammo not included! You recall that for your prom, you borrowed your Uncle Lenny's 1983 Chrysler Imperial. Looking back on it now, you realize what a geeky choice that was. But then again, it was certainly comfortable enough for you and Irene when the two of you . . .

A half hour later, your son returns home with his date, Heather, for pictures. As your wife snaps away, you're surprised at how attractive Heather is. The few times you've met her, she was wearing a hooded sweatshirt and jeans. But seeing her in a dress you realize that your son is doing A-OK!

As they head out, you say, "Have fun!" and wink at him slyly.

"Oh, we will," he says with a mischievous smile and a thumbs-up.

As you and your wife stand on your front porch and watch them drive away in a vehicle that would normally be preceded by a minesweeper, you realize that your little boy is well on his way to becoming a young man . . . just like you were that night with Irene Castagnola.

But if you are the father of a daughter you will see things so very differently. First, when the subject of her attending the prom comes up, you are dead set against it. Instead of wasting all that money on just one night, you suggest that she commit herself to something more lasting, more rewarding . . . like a convent.

But you know there's no stopping it, so instead of renting a limo—which these days seems to be as necessary a prom accessory as a corsage—you suggest that *you* drive your daughter and her date. This idea, of course, is met with immediate ridicule; your daughter says that she and her boyfriend have reputations to uphold, and they don't want their street cred getting torpedoed by a guy in his bathrobe and slippers, flashing his headlights at midnight in the school parking lot.

So you decide to calm down . . . let it go . . . it's just a prom, right? What's the worst that could happen?

"How do I look, Daddy?" she asks as she comes out of her bedroom with her mother.

As you turn to look at her, only two words occur to you: *holy crap!* Who is this gorgeous person? And what are those things on her chest that are trying to tickle her chin? Her dress makes her look ten years older. And her legs six inches longer. Does it have to be so short? She looks absolutely stunning! She should be a runway model! Runway model, hell! She should be in the Parcheesi Club!

"Daddy?" she asks again.

"Oh, Gina, you look absolutely terrific. What are you planning to wear as a jacket?"

"Jacket? Daddy, it's almost summer."

You look to your wife for help, but all you get is a proud smile that says, "See? I told you this would happen someday, but you wouldn't listen, would you?"

So all you can say to your daughter is, "So, you're going out just like that?"

"Well, I'm taking a clutch purse," she says.

As you stare at her, you think about the little girl who used to pretend to be a waitress and serve you scribbled eggs. Where did she go?

Then your doorbell rings.

Your wife opens it to your daughter's boyfriend, a tall, gangly kid named Gary.

"Hi, Mrs. Johnson," he says. Then he looks to you. "Mr. Johnson, sir. How are you?"

But before you can say, "I'd be a helluva lot better if my daughter's dress covered more of her," Gary sets his eyes on her.

"Wow," he says, grabbing hold of a chair in case he should faint dead away.

Your daughter smiles at him; this is just the reaction she was looking for. After Gary recovers whatever senses a boy who enjoys going to water polo practice at six in the morning might possess, he goes to your daughter to present her with a corsage.

"Here, Gina," he says. As he contemplates a place to pin it, he gets dangerously close to receiving a head slap from you.

"Maybe your mom should do this," he finally concedes.

As your wife applies the corsage, Gary informs you of the night's plans. After the prom, a group is going to a pricey restaurant for a late-night dinner, followed by a few parties.

"But don't worry, Mr. Johnson, I don't drink."

You genuinely appreciate him broaching that subject, and you tell him so. Then, when you consider that your daughter will be out for most of the night wearing a dress like that, it's likely that you will be doing enough drinking for the both of you.

As your wife poses them for pictures, you begin to get an image of something . . . something very unsettling. But you're not sure what it is. But then, as Gary puts his arm around your daughter's waist, and she presses herself close to him, it hits you. Your prom night with Irene Castagnola! My God, the similarities are paralyzing! Gina and Gary have been dating for about six months, just like you and Irene were. Gary is wearing black tuxedo pants and a white dinner jacket, and Gina is wearing a black dress with a bow . . . just like you and Irene did!

"So, did you rent a limo?" you mumble to Gary, as if you'd just suffered a minor stroke.

"No, sir," he answers. "My uncle Jim is in the classic car business. He lent me a totally cherry 1983 Chrysler Imperial."

Your head spins; you feel so flush that you're completely unaware that the photo session has ended and this Gary fellow is leading your precious daughter toward the door.

"Good night, Daddy," she says, only blowing you a kiss so as not to smudge her makeup.

"Huh? Oh, yeah. Night."

As they start out, you come to your senses enough to hurry after them. "Hey, Gar!" you call, pulling him aside.

"Yes, Mr. Johnson?" he asks confidentially.

"Look, I just want you to know that I hope you two have a very nice time tonight."

"Thank you, sir," he says.

"And I want you to know one other thing."

"What's that, sir?"

You stare him squarely in the eye. "I know where you live."

And then you give him a way-too-firm slap on the back and send him on his way.

Much later that night, you are sitting in your easy chair, fighting to stay awake as you think about your daughter, Gary, and that damn Chrysler Imperial.

"C'mon, Ed, let's turn in," your wife says. "It's nearly two-thirty."

"But I wanted to wait up for Gina."

"I already told you. She and Gary and a bunch of other kids are at Mike and Joyce Rapperwill's house. They're all going to see how long they can stay awake, and Joyce is fixing everyone breakfast."

"The Rapperwills? Are they OK?"

"They're both police officers. I think the kids are safe there."

You sigh and head for the bedroom with your wife.

Forty-five minutes later, you are still awake.

"Ed, sweetie, try to get to sleep, OK?"

"Yeah, OK," you sigh. Your wife, as usual, knows exactly what you're thinking.

"She's not a baby anymore," she says.

"Tell me about it," you say.

Then you kiss warmly, she rolls over on her side and you wrap your arms around her.

After a moment, she says, "I sure love you, Ed."

"Oh, I love you more, Irene."

And soon, you are both asleep.

FIFTEEN

GOING ... GOING ... GONE!

Well, you made it. Even before the last note of "Pomp and Circumstance" faded into the June air above your child's high school football field, you heaved a huge sigh of relief. And you should; it's quite an accomplishment getting a child this far.

By graduation, your child has probably reached the age of eighteen—or soon will—which means he or she is considered a legal adult. What this represents to you is that your "little baby" is now old enough to do wonderful things like vote, apply for a loan without you as a co-signer, and rent an apartment with its own washer and dryer, located at least thirty minutes from your house. Suddenly, you feel a huge weight lifted from your shoulders.

For many, this will be the last summer your child lives at home before going off to college, joining the military, or perhaps getting a full-time job and moving in with friends. So you will not only be saying good-bye to your child, but also to a sink full of dirty dishes when the dishwasher is empty, one sheet remaining on the toilet paper roll, an empty gas tank, and strangers peering into your refrigerator like it's a plasma screen. To all that, you can say, "Adios!"

And in the next breath, you can say "hello" to the wonderful silence that used to exist in your home before you decided to bring a mini-you into it.

And although you have been looking forward to the day when you can once again spend Saturday mornings parading around your house in your favorite ripped boxers, your wife is not likely to feel the same way. And this is not just because you outgrew those boxers years ago, and what she has to look at when you pass by makes her want to remove her eyes with white-hot barbecue tongs.

Your wife's fear is that she is losing grasp of the person to whom she has basically dedicated her life to for the past eighteen years; so she may be a little bit down for the first few days. We suggest you be extra attentive and do whatever she asks of you . . . short of accompanying her to a Jane Austen Film Festival, of course. We also recommend that, if one of these first few days falls on a Saturday, you keep your old boxers in the drawer. This is not only out of consideration for your wife, but also for your own safety. Or have you forgotten all about Lorena Bobbitt?

But after only a few short days, your wife will brighten when she realizes that she's speaking to your moved-out child more often than when he or she lived at home. If it's your daughter who recently moved away for college, the two of them will talk at least twice a day, and their conversations will usually be "girl talk," rather than something specific. Your wife is thrilled because they never talked this much at home without it ending in a door being slammed.

If it's your son away at college, his calls will be frequent as well, but will be more curious, yet practical, in nature. Like asking what microwave setting he should use to warm his socks; if $12 is too much to spend for a used sofa; and what is the name of the stuff she used to get dog barf out of the carpet?

And it's only a matter of time before your wife will be as excited as you are about your regained independence; before you know it, you will be sleeping late on weekends, with or without pajamas; you will go days at a time without once hearing the word "dude"; you'll be blasting your kind of music, which means "Hello, Dr. Dre! Goodbye, Dr. John!"

And before long, your life will be yours again!

But before you trade in your "World's Greatest Dad" hat for a do-rag that'll look really cool on you behind the wheel of that sporty little convertible you've had your eye on, remember this rule: you never retire from being a dad.

Oh, sure, you can retire from being a policeman or a teacher, a donut maker or a preacher. If you choose, you can stop being a husband, or a golfer, or a smoker. But you cannot stop being a dad.

"Hey, Stan, it's been a while. How are your children doing?"

"Children? Oh, no, I got out of that a couple of years ago. I'm raising Airedale terriers now."

Because the truth is, no matter how old your kids are, or how long they've been gone, there is always a possibility that, at some point, they will need to return. It doesn't matter if you change your locks, your security code, your address, or your identity . . . they will seek you out when they have nowhere else to turn. And you will welcome them back with open arms, because you're a wonderful human being, right? Because you missed them so much, correct? Who are you trying to kid, cowboy? You let them move back home because your wife said so.

So get used to it.

It could happen right after college, because after four to six years of parties, intramural sports, sororities, and changing majors, they are "wiped out, bro." They need a place to chart their future—a place that's quiet, a place that's familiar, a place that's free.

Or maybe they'll knock on your door a few years later, when their dream job turns into a nightmare.

"Hi, honey. How was your trip?" your wife asks as soon as you walk in from a three-day sales meeting. She has a Scotch on the rocks already prepared for you. That's not normal.

"Same ole, same ole," you answer. You study the drink for a moment. "Something up?"

"Well, Danny called while you were gone. . . . " From the somber tone of her voice, you say a quick prayer that—whatever your unmarried, twenty-six-year-old son had to say—the next sentence doesn't contain the words "totaled," "bail," or "I swear she looked over eighteen."

"And?" you say, suddenly hoping that there's more Scotch left.

"He lost his job."

"What? Why? I thought he was doing great."

"Yeah, well, he and his boss had a disagreement."

"Did he say about what?"

"Uh-huh. Danny called his boss a raving, lunatic butt head. Apparently his boss disagreed."

"Oh, excellent move. This isn't the best time to be job hunting . . . even with a degree."

"Well, he thinks he'll be able to find something . . . eventually."

"Eventually? What's he gonna do *now*?"

"Well, we talked, and . . . " Before she finishes, there's a knock on the front door.

Your wife hurries to get it, but you're closer and get there first. What's her hurry, you wonder?

When you open the door, an explanation begins to form. Your son is there; he's lugging two suitcases and his laptop. Perched on his head is a sombrero embroidered "Ensenada,

Spring Break 2005." This is troublesome enough, but as you look past him to the street, your heart drops. Parked out front, you see the new car he bought just a month ago, thanks to his "job security." Attached to his car is a U-Haul trailer overflowing with things that look vaguely familiar to you. That's because most of those things used to be in your house.

But that was before you remodeled.

And before you turned his bedroom into a wine tasting room.

"Hi, Dad," he says, waving his keys. "I see you changed the locks."

You down your Scotch.

The following Saturday morning, you are not lazing in your old boxers. Instead, you and your son are carrying bottles of cabernet and pinot grigio out of what used to be his old room, and what will soon be your old wine cellar.

And that's what you do on Sunday, too.

Sunday evening you are exhausted from getting your new, old roommate settled. You stand under a hot shower for so long that you look like an eighty-year-old lobster. As you put on a sweat suit and slippers, your son calls through the door.

"Dad, you in there?"

"Yeah, c'mon in," you say.

He walks in, carrying a bottle of wine. "Here," he says, handing it to you. "I was going to give it to you for your birthday, but . . . "

You check the label and are immediately impressed.

"Jeez, Danny, you shouldn't have spent so much. This is . . . "

"Dad, c'mon. I had a job, remember?"

"Yeah."

He falls silent for a minute, his eyes on the floor. Then when he looks up, they've moistened a bit. "Look, Dad, I won't be here long. Promise."

You see that he's hurting, and then you see something else: your adult son is scared to death.

"What are you talking about? This is your house, too," you tell him, a good part of you hoping that he doesn't take you literally. Then you put your arm around his shoulder. "Hey, it'll be nice having you around for awhile."

"You mean it?" he asks, finally allowing himself to smile.

"Of course I mean it," you say gregariously.

And you know what? You do.

SIXTEEN

CREATIVE EMBARRASSMENT

Every dad with a starter-set of Father's Day ties knows that it is not easy to get your children to do something they do not want to do. We believe that there are two underlying reasons for this:

1) Although on a much smaller scale, children don't want to do the same types of things that adults don't want to do.

2) Getting a child to do something is easier if that child trusts you completely. But because parents violate this sacred trust very early on, it's not hard to understand why. As a child gets older, he doesn't want to do something even less than when he didn't want to do it in the first place.

You with us so far? Good.

Let's start with the "trust" thing first. From the time human children are conceived, they rely on their mother for nourishment. And for nearly nine months, their mother delivers, and these tummy-dwellers learn to trust that their mother will provide what they need. But then, when babies emerge from the womb, they are hit with a whole new way of eating. "Hey, what's going on here? I trusted you! I . . . " But then, before they can gripe any further, something is popped into their mouth and they are introduced to their mother's breast or to a bottle, which they take to immediately and enthusiastically. "Wow, this is a lot more fun than getting fed through my belly button! And it tastes

great, too! I knew I could trust her." But can you imagine what a violation of that trust it would be if mothers' milk didn't appeal to babies? What if it tasted like, say, sauerkraut, or deep-fried mackerel, or even Jimmy Dean's pork sausage (the patties, not the links; the links are awesome)? What do you suppose a baby would think?

"Hey, what's up with this? I trusted you!"

But because mother's milk is pure and exactly what the baby needs, this bond of trust remains strong.

Until about six months later, when it's time to wean our infant from milk onto solid foods. We try to feed it to him directly on a small spoon, but just the aroma of pabulum, or cooked carrots, or pureed chicken makes him turn his head and tighten his lips. So what do we do? We put the spoon up to our mouths and pretend to eat something that looks like it belongs in a litter box. "Mmmmm-mmmmmm," we say. "Daddy thinks this is so yummy! And you trust Daddy, don't you?"

The baby stares at you, thinking, "You know . . . I don't trust him like I trust the pretty one with the long hair and no beer breath . . . but she seems to trust him, so what the heck?" So he slowly opens his mouth and you shove in a spoonful of stewed brussels sprouts. And no sooner does he close his mouth than he opens it again to spit up all over your eyeglasses.

But he's not just spitting out the food, he's spitting out every ounce of trust he had in you. And that trust is hard, if not impossible, to win back. And as your baby grows older, he becomes even more distrustful because some of the stunts you pull.

"C'mon, Claire, jump!" you say to your three-year-old daughter who stands on the edge of a swimming pool. You are waist-deep in the water, holding out your arms for her. "You can do it, honey. It's not cold," you reassure her between your shivers. And finally, after some more gentle prodding, she takes the plunge.

As soon as she hits the water, it's "Waaahhhh!", and the only warm water comes from the tears that instantaneously begin rolling down her cheeks.

Guess what, Dad? It's hello, goose bumps, good-bye trust.

Your ten-year-old-son is at bat in a baseball game. You're his coach and you shout out instructions. "Move closer to the plate, Jeff!" The frightened child moves about half a millimeter nearer. "More than that, Son! Don't be afraid of the ball! It won't hurt you!"

Not more than five seconds later, he is on the ground, writhing, because the pitcher arced one a bit inside and it bounced off his upper arm. He collapsed as if he'd been felled by a buffalo gun and is screaming like he'd just had his appendix removed with a knitting needle and a pair of vise grips.

You run out, pick him up, and dust him off. "You OK?"

"Won't hurt, huh?" he says between sobs. "Thanks a lot, Dad!"

And as he staggers toward first base, he takes his trust with him.

And the final straw could very well be when you assure your seventeen-year-old daughter that having her impacted wisdom teeth removed will be relatively painless, and that she'll able to eat all the ice cream and drink all the malts she wants to afterward.

"It still hurts like hell, Dad," she mumbles three days after surgery through swollen jaws stuffed with gauze. "And if I have another bowl of ice cream, I'm gonna barf."

So that pretty much exhausts the "trust me" approach of getting your children to do things they don't want to do.

The second method is negotiation/reward, like, "If you wash the car, I'll let you drive it tonight." But deals like this will only work a few times before kids figure out how to get what they want without having to perform any services. "Never mind. Ted's gonna drive. His tires aren't *that* bald."

So, with the "trust me" and the "negotiation" approaches in the shredder, most dads find themselves resorting to the "threat" technique. "If you don't bring home at least a 3.0 this semester, you will not drive for a month." But even the most strident dads see that this approach quickly becomes toothless when your daughter brings home a report card with a GPA of 2.8.

"OK, give me your keys," you say to her firmly. "Hope you have a bus pass." She casually removes her keys from her purse and hands them to you. You think you detect an eye roll and a suppressed smile. What's with her, you wonder? Does she think I'm kidding about this?

An hour later, you are trying to fix some spaghetti for dinner because your wife is working late. You look at your watch. Uh-oh, you completely forgot about something. "Cynthia, I need you to pick up your brother from his tuba lesson," you say to your daughter at the kitchen table, where she's doing her homework.

"Like to, Dad, but I can't drive," she answers. "Maybe next month."

You think about this for a moment; you can't just give in. It's important that you have the last word.

"OK," you say as you toss her the keys. "But next semester, I want at least a 2.9, understand?"

And that is that.

So once you've tried everything in your repertoire to get your kids to do things they don't want to do, then what?

We suggest what we call "creative embarrassment," which is based on every dad's knowledge that all children hate being embarrassed, and will do almost anything to avoid it. And, like in any situation where you are facing a formidable opponent, you are allowed to exploit any of their weaknesses. You should know, however, that this method takes a certain amount of courage from you, as you may be embarrassing yourself as well. But considering your golf game, you should be used to that. But you'll forget all about this when you see your child's face turn the color of a freshly sliced tomato.

Here are a couple of examples of creative embarrassment, just to get you started. . . .

The first one will work on any misbehaving son as young as eight or daughter as young as four, and needs very little, if any, preparation. The only requirement is that you and your family occasionally attend church. (Note: This example will normally work on any day of worship; but if you're not a regular churchgoer, a major religious holiday is always good.)

This method is effective in a cathedral, synagogue, mosque, or whatever. But for this example, we'll say it's Christmas morning (or the comparable winter solstice holiday) and you and your family are in a Lutheran church. The leader of the ceremony announces that the first song will be "Silent Night," and he encourages the entire congregation to sing along.

After a short organ intro, everyone begins tentatively. But not you, who come out of the box singing with gusto you've never before displayed. "Silent night, holy night, all is calm"—you croon with the verve of an *American Idol* hopeful—"all is bright." You look down at your eight-year-old son, who's noticeably uncomfortable by now, but not quite blushing yet. This means you need to kick it up a notch, so you deepen your voice to an operatic tone and volume. "Round yon virgin, mother and child; holy infant . . . " By this time, people around you will be trying to sneak a peek at the yahoo who thinks he's Placido Domingo. Your son notices this, too, and tugs on your jacket.

"Dad!" he whispers.

When you look down, you see that his face is the color of Rudolph's nose.

"Yeah?"

"Could you sing a little quieter?" he begs.

"Oh, sure," you say.

And voila! You've hooked yourself a fish. Now you just have to reel him in, which you can do whenever you choose. Let's say it's a Saturday, and the whole family knows you'll be going to church tomorrow. As you pass through the room, your wife is asking your son to please clean his room. He whines, scowls, and puts up an overall stink. He folds his arms, defiant, and plops down on the couch; it appears there will be no bedroom cleaning today.

Then you suddenly begin belting out, in your finest *La Traviata* basso, the lyrics to "Silent Night." When your wife turns to you, you stop your singing just long enough to say, "Oh, sorry, honey, just getting ready for church tomorrow."

Then, after you make a short and simple pact with your son, he hurries in to clean his room.

And Mario Lanza retires until he's needed again.

The point is this: All you need to do is find out what embarrasses your child the most, and then go for it. And remember, teenagers are the ones who most care about what people think of them; therefore, they fear being embarrassed by you even more than being caught with a John Tesh CD.

Here's an example of how a dad can use creative embarrassment to gain an upper hand on his teenager.

Carl, the father of a seventeen-year-old girl, walks into a heated discussion between his daughter and his wife about the teenager's outfit as she waits for her date to arrive. Carl's wife is adamant that the girl's skirt is too short, and her neckline too revealing.

"Do you expect me to allow you to go out dressed like that?" Carl's wife yells.

"You are so out of it," their daughter snaps back. "Why is it that I'm the only one in this house who can't dress the way she wants?"

Then she strikes "The Pose," a popular, in-your-face move that teenage girls use to show their defiance. First, she stiffens her right leg and puts all her weight on it, which causes her right hip and buttock to jut out just a bit. Then she bends her left leg at the knee and touches her left ankle to her right ankle, forming a figure 4. Then she folds her arms tightly against her chest to complete the maneuver.

Her mom stares at her, then turns to Carl. "What do you think?" she asks her husband.

Carl sighs. "I hate to take sides, but I agree with Tess," he says to his wife. "Why should she be the only one in the house who can't dress the way she wants?"

As Carl's wife tightens her jaw, the teenager smiles at her father. "Thank you, Daddy," she says to him as he goes back into his bedroom. Then Tess shoots her mother a victorious smile.

Seven minutes later, the doorbell rings. But before his daughter or his wife can answer it, Carl bolts out of his bedroom, wearing nothing but a pair of underwear, a T-shirt that he has fashioned into a crop top, rain boots, and a fishing hat.

"Daddy!" his daughter screeches. "What are you doing?"

"I'm going to answer the door," he says innocently. "I want to meet your date."

"Daddy, not like that!" she screams, covering her eyes.

"Why not? I've always wanted to dress like this. And in this house, no one should tell me how to dress, right?"

He grabs the doorknob and starts to turn it.

"OK!" Tess finally says, relenting. Then she hurries into her bedroom to change.

After Carl gives his wife a quick kiss and scampers back to his bedroom, she answers the door and invites Tess's date in. They have a nice chat before she comes out from her room, dressed in a longer skirt and a sweater.

And from that night on, whenever Carl or his wife thought Tess was dressed improperly, all he had to do was put on his fishing hat.

Case closed.

SEVENTEEN

GET BACK ON THE HORSE ... BUT NO GALLOPING!

Because the divorce rate in the United States currently hovers right around 50 percent, there's a 1 in 2 chance that a married dad may someday find himself as a single dad. In most divorces where children are involved, primary custody is awarded to the mother, which means most divorced dads will see their children mainly on weekends. If you're in this group, we'll get to you soon. But for a moment, let's talk about fathers who *are* awarded custody of their children. Bless you, guys, but do you have a lot to learn! And fast, because your workload just more than doubled. *Way* more. You will immediately realize that you just may have underestimated the role of teamwork in raising kids.

It's like spending a tennis career playing doubles; you focus on strategy and maximizing the different strengths of both partners. You specialize in deep ground strokes, powerful overheads, or the finesse of the drop shot, while your partner's strengths are serving, backhands, and covering the baseline. But suddenly you're playing singles, and it's a different game—all speed and stamina, both of which you lost in Mario's Italian Kitchen about fifteen years and thirty pounds ago.

Or say you're a tag-team wrestler. When your opponent, a 275-pound failed actor loaded with steroids, has you in a reverse death pretzel, you claw your way to the ropes for the tag so your partner can launch a flying pile driver onto your adversary. But when you're a single dad, and your six-year-old has you locked up in a step-over guilt trip, or your teenager has paralyzed you with her nineteenth assurance that day that you have ruined her life, there is no folding chair with which you can defend yourself. You realize that trying to be a one-man band is extremely difficult, particularly in a situation where an orchestra would work much better.

So you dig in and try to work out an efficient way to balance your work, the kids' school, and their playdates. In the beginning, things are excruciatingly difficult. You dream of a thirty-hour day and bemoan that a reliable cloning technique has not yet been perfected. You are sleep deprived, overworked, and cranky all the time—just like when your kids were first born. Except now they eat more, do less, and are not nearly as cute. But eventually—with your kids' help—you learn to make adjustments, and things settle into a livable, if chaotic, pattern. You are finally getting your feet back under you, and most of the time your kids are clean and well fed, meaning they no longer look like poster children for a Doctors Without Borders brochure.

And along with a growing sense of domestic tranquility, you will begin to find time to read, to watch television, and to wonder where the hell your life is going. It's then that you begin to have stirrings that you haven't had in a while; and even if you had, you wouldn't have had the time to do anything about them. But now, whether you have your kids 24/7 or just on an occasional weekend, it becomes apparent even to them, who often notice you smiling sheepishly at attractive women in the supermarket or the mall. When they tease you about it, you dismiss it, saying they're imagining things. But you know better, and when you catch yourself ogling women in the carpool lane, just out of bed, in their rumpled sweat suits and uncombed hair tucked under a ball cap, you realize that it's time for you to get back in the game.

The problem is, you've been on the sidelines for so long that you're no longer sure of the rules. But you suspect that your old moves from back in the day—which, even you admit, weren't very smooth to begin with—may not get you where you want to go. You are pretty confident that your letterman sweater is no longer the aphrodisiac you always thought it was. And your old strategy of driving by a girl's house in the middle of the night and revving your engine may have lost some of its magic . . . particularly since you own a four-year-old hybrid. And if restraining orders were once an ordinary part of your courting rituals, it is definitely time to develop a new game plan.

You don't know where to start. If you invite a woman out for a movie, will she laugh in your face because she already watched it on her phone? Maybe you should find a nice bar where you could meet someone; after all, that's how you hooked up with your ex-wife.

OK, so bars are out.

You consider some of the places friends have suggested: The PTA. Bingo night. Laundromat. The produce section of any supermarket. Finally, a friend from work suggests that you join the local food co-op. It's nonthreatening; it's chockablock full with women; and it has the collateral advantage of providing healthy food for the family.

You investigate and find out the co-op meets every two weeks, which gives you plenty of time to brush up on organic vegetables, socialism, and folk music. You arrive a little late to find everyone sitting together, talking over the healthiest options for upcoming meals and the economic value of buying in bulk.

You also realize that your friend from work was right . . . there are about fifteen women and only two men other than yourself; you may have struck the mother lode and you are a father! You settle back in your chair and occasionally pipe in with things like: "Yep, the times, they are a-changin'" and, "Give a man endive and you feed him for a day; teach a man how to grow endive and you feed him for a lifetime." Then you add something that you thought up on the drive over. "And he won't weigh much, either!" When this doesn't collect the laugh you thought it should, you begin to look at these women in a different light, and it isn't long before you see that many of them fit a certain profile. Wanda spent seven weeks in a redwood tree, protesting clear-cutting in Oregon; Rainbow bears the unmistakable odor of the free-range chickens she raises in her backyard; and BethAnn only wears jewelry made of shallots. Including you and the two other guys, there's not a shaved armpit in the group. But you're determined to stick with it, and even go so far as to invest in a whole new wardrobe, featuring Eddie Bauer chamois shirts, cargo pants, and Birkenstock sandals. But before these purchases can yield any dividends, your kids protest that they can't face another veggie burger, yogurt pop, or lactose-free tofu bar, and that they will never drink the goat's milk that's beginning to go "baaaaaad" in your fridge. You decide that the co-op isn't for you, but are a bit afraid to face the ladies in person, so you tender your resignation via cell phone from the supermarket, where you're stocking up on fried pork rinds, Hawaiian punch, and Ho Hos.

After several weeks of eating junk food and wallowing in the failure of your first attempt at reentering the courting world, the TV show *The Biggest Loser* is starting to hit a little too close to home. You've had to dump the cargo pants in favor of the more forgiving Sansabelt waistlines. And while your T-shirts have become fashionably tight, you find that when you lean way back on your sofa, you're sporting an unintentional bare midriff look, only without the navel piercing. And finally, when you pop a button on your Relaxed Fit Levis, you come to the realization that you can either invest in an entire wardrobe of dashikis, or look into an exercise plan. But let's face it—you have the will power of an alcoholic at Oktoberfest, so you need someone who will *force* you to exercise. That very evening as you're leafing through the sports page, you see an ad for something that you hope will change your life in more ways than one. Body Blast Boot Camp is opening a new facility nearby, and they are offering free initiation with a one-year commitment. You wash down your Twinkie with a slug of Mountain Dew, reach for the phone, and schedule a consultation.

"Hi, Herb, my name's Bambi and I'll be your guide," says the fitness instructor who greets you when you arrive. You shake hands with a woman who is so fit and so toned that your intimidated and defensive male ego tells you that she *must* have an errant Y chromosome lurking somewhere in her enormous pythons, even though her voluptuous body and extremely gorgeous face suggest otherwise. You follow Bambi past the juice bar, back through the weight room; you tour the locker room, the classrooms, and the pool. From time to time, you even look up from Bambi's Body Blasted booty to survey what's going on in the gym. You're impressed! How, you wonder, do some of these very fit and attractive women get into their shorts without WD-40 and a carpet stretcher? You decide that this is the perfect time for you to take control of your life and assume your rightful place among these chiseled gods and goddesses. Get ready spandex, here you come!

Four weeks later, you're on the treadmill, watching Home Shopping Network on a bank of TVs. It's a beautiful Saturday afternoon, and you wonder why you're inside, paying to walk in place like a hamster in a wheel, instead of power walking down the boardwalk, looking for a place to have a pastrami on rye and a brewski.

While your mind wanders, all the people around you—a lot of them women—are on their treadmills, reading books or magazines, seemingly very focused on their workouts. You've tried to keep interested, and even participated in some of the classes the gym offers. You've found that hot yoga leaves you cold, and kickboxing has confirmed what you suspected when you first walked in the gym—that every woman there can likely kick your ass. You were able to strike up a conversation with some of these gals, most of whom are very attractive, but it usually led to their split times in the pool or their triglyceride levels. You haven't been able to sit up in bed for two weeks, or to tie your own shoes for a month.

You finally are forced to admit defeat, but reason that at least you didn't waste the money on the gym's initiation fee, while conveniently overlooking the year's worth of dues you're now stuck with. Perhaps you'll give your membership to your younger brother.

Once you've exhausted every other option, from the line-dancing classes to the book club to your tonal meditation group, there is but one alternative for you to try, and it's probably the one you should have tried first.

So wax your (key)board, bro! You're going surfing!

EIGHTEEN

GENTLEMEN, START YOUR (SEARCH) ENGINES

OK, because your last *real* date was so long ago that you wore a Nehru jacket, we know how your old-fashioned mind works. When you think Campbell's, you think soup; when you think Ed McMahon, you think Johnny Carson. When you think Elvis Presley, you think, "Damn, I could use a pie." And when you think Internet dating, you think, "Loser!"

Well, shake loose those chains, my bell-bottomed friend. We're ten years into the new millennium; it's time you emerge from your cave and join the rest of us. Granted, when Internet dating was born over fifteen years ago, it may have had a certain aura of abject desperation about it. In fact, many couples who met via the Internet back then were too embarrassed to admit it.

It's 1996, and Bob is at a party with his wife, Ruth, whom he met via the Internet. "So, Bob, how did you and the missus meet?" someone asks him casually. Bob and Ruth exchange embarrassed glances. Bob finally speaks.

"Oh, it wasn't all that hard," Bob says. "We're cousins."

But in today's climate of go-go social networking, Internet dating has emerged as a respectable and invaluable time-saving tool to cast a net so large that if you can't find someone compatible with you, you better put your fishing pole on ice, because you won't be needing it.

And while many Web matchmaking services are general in nature, there are hundreds of sites that can find very specific fits for their clients. Looking for a left-handed insurance actuary who likes Frisbee, has a gluten allergy, and enjoys the music of the Kinks? No problemo. How about a myopic philatelist who loves hang gliding and pomegranates? Got a half dozen. You name the permutation, and there is surely someone out there who is a perfect fit for you. So successful is the Internet in matching people that it is estimated that one out of five marriages today result from Internet social networking.

So grab that mouse, big guy, and find yourself some cheese.

But in case you don't know where to begin, here are tips to help you get started. Once you select a Web site that you think you'd be comfortable with, you'll need to create a screen name for yourself. Ideally, a screen name gives an intriguing hint of what you're all about. For example, let's say you're in the moving business; perhaps a screen name like "IwillmoveU" might work just fine. However, something like "BigChestGrabber" may not fill the bill. Or perhaps, if you're an avid golfer, "LuvBirdies" would suit you, whereas "LongStiffShaft" is probably something you should reconsider.

Along with your screen name, you'll also need a picture. A word of warning: do not put up a picture of yourself that is any more than a year old. Keep in mind that the object of this whole exercise is to form a relationship, not show up at her house for the first time and have her laugh you off her front porch.

If, however, you feel insecure about some part of your appearance, it is perfectly acceptable to try to draw one's attention away from your flaw. For example, if you have a nose the size of an overgrown cucumber, you might want to perch a colorful parrot on it, and have your picture taken while sitting in a tree, with the hope that interested females will mistake your honker for just another branch.

Another surefire way to make up for your perceived lack of hotness—or even if you're so handsome that you make Brad Pitt look like Rush Limbaugh—is to include your dog in your picture. Women dig animals almost as much as they dig men who dig animals. If you don't have a dog, rent one. We know you think this could get dicey. After all, what happens if you land a date with your dream woman and you end up at your place? What are you going to say about your dog?

"He died," you tell her, fighting back tears.

"Oh, I'm sorry," she says. "When?"

"This morning," you say, barely able to speak.

"What? And you still kept our date?"

"Hey," you tell her. "It's not every day a guy gets a chance to be with someone so special. I just wish Rex had been here to meet you!"

(Note: Beforehand, you should spend a few dollars on some used doggy toys and place them around your house. You should also knot up your crustiest sweat sock and wedge it between your sofa cushions.)

Then you become so bereft, that you crumble onto your sofa. She will likely join you, wanting to do whatever she can to console you. It's here that you reach between the cushions and happen to retrieve Rex's favorite plaything . . . one of your old socks. You are now so overcome with loss that she will likely caress you, burying your head in the softness of her neck.

You're halfway home, my friend. Now all you have to do is make up a story about that nose.

NINETEEN

MAY TO DECEMBER AND BACK AGAIN

Once you take the plunge back into the dating pool, you will find that age is a lot less important than it was years ago. Today's older people are looking a lot younger than older people looked thirty years ago. Think back to your parents, grandparents, aunts, and uncles. . . . When they were forty, they moved like they were fifty; when they were fifty-five, they moved like they were seventy. And when they were sixty-five, they moved to Boca Raton. That's because they wanted to be with other old people who walked old, talked old, and smelled old. But as we like to say today, sixty is the new forty; fifty is the new thirty-five; forty is the new thirty! We suspect that this is why the "new math" has become so popular—it was likely conceived by a sixty-five-year-old who'd had three chin tucks.

The point is, whether we attribute it to improved health habits, medical advances, or elective surgeries, today we are living longer and looking younger, which means the span between baby diapers and adult diapers keeps getting greater and greater.

And with the divorce rate being what it is, there are more beautiful, sexy, vibrant, intelligent, and available women in their forties, fifties, and sixties who would make wonderful life partners for men of the same age. But for some reason, there are still, unfortunately, a number of older, unenlightened, Neanderthals who choose to over-look these exquisite jewels in favor of much, much younger women.

To men like this, we say: "Shame on you!"

But only when our wives are with us.

If you're considering a serious relationship with a woman who's, say, twenty-six, the first thing you should realize is that the new math we just talked about really makes her about seventeen and a half, two years younger than your daughter. (Just trying to make it easier for you.)

You see nothing out of the ordinary about the age differ-ence, because you consider yourself, at worst, a "middle-aged man" (i.e., forty to fifty for most guys, unless you're an actor or a New York real estate billionaire with really bad hair. These folks consider "middle age" to be anywhere between fifty-five and ninety-two.). It's probable that you were previously married to a woman your own age who, like you, believed that playing "You Light Up My Life" at your wedding guaranteed a lifetime of happiness.

And maybe it has . . . just not with each other.

Let's say, after considering all the ramifications and procuring a healthy supply of miracle pharmaceuticals to insure that all your equipment is functioning at peak capacity, you decide to go for it. The two of you fall madly in love and set a date for your wedding. Your daughter isn't thrilled, but eventually comes to accept it, attributing it to her "crazy old father," the same guy who wore underpants and a fishing hat to embarrass her when she was younger.

Soon after your marriage, your new wife's nesting instinct comes into play and she begins talking about starting a family. This is because she realizes that at your age, not only is your biological clock losing time, but your watchband may be sprung and your gears are almost stripped. And sure enough, it isn't long before you're wandering the aisles of a baby warehouse, just like you did twenty years earlier. As your beautiful wife shows her excitement and youthful enthusiasm over everything baby, you eyes are glued to your iPhone, where you're streaming the Senior PGA Championship.

As you move into the crib and bassinette section you smile at the irony . . . when the two of you first hooked up, you would often go to this rather kinky lingerie shop she knew of, where you would buy lace bras, teddies, and edible panties. Now you are in Babies"R"Us, shopping for Winnie-the-Pooh mobiles and a Happy Princess diaper bag.

When your baby is born, you are thrilled, even though you know you have to go through the whole "dad" thing once again. And as your child grows, you will have to learn to keep your cool when soccer parents exclaim, "Oh that's nice. Little Jamie's grandfather brought her to the game today." But you'll get used to it, because the same thing will happen on the ski slopes, in the mall, and at Back to School Night.

But there is a bright side to the situation: As your children move into their teen years, their friends will covet your collection of "classic" music, and they will often seek your knowledge of events of historical significance, like the disco era. Also, your closet will become a rich source of costumes for their parties, and you will often hear the words "old school" and "retro" to describe everything about you, from your comfy Velcro shoes all the way up to your fishing hat.

But the fact that you're willing to undertake this kind of challenge suggests that you enjoy being a dad and are equal to the task in all regards. Or that you are too old to realize the peril and it won't even register.

Either way, you'll be OK. Good luck and be secure in the knowledge that most high school graduations offer wheelchair ramps and salt-free snacks.

★ ★ ★

But what if one of these aforementioned knockout forty- to sixty-year-old women takes an interest in poor, defenseless, little thirty-five-year-old you?

And then, what if the feeling is likewise?

Could happen, because with the advent of the fifty-year-old pregnant woman, the older man/younger woman paradigm certainly has a "B" side. Women who have battled it out in work, marriage, and the equality debate are finally coming into their own. The term "cougar" has entered our vocabulary to describe women who, like their male counterparts, have scored a sexual hat trick by developing a career, dumping the old man, and lassoing a younger one to accompany them into the "heeee-yaahhh!" phase of their lives.

And what if one of these young studs is you? Of course, you'll be wondering, "Am I just a piece of meat? Just some nachos on her combination plate of love?" You might even feel dirty . . . used and abused, just because you have wash-board abs, perfectly straight teeth, and a killer sense of style. But that doesn't mean you're nothing more than arm candy, does it? Of course not. You really like her, and she feels the same about you. So you keep on seeing each other and eventually you tie the knot.

As a trophy husband, you will need to be on call at all times, but this will not likely cut into your golf and tennis time at your new country club. We also advise you to continue with your career, even though your new bride thinks there's not much of a future in driving a bread delivery truck. Just because she is a trust-funded corporate titan, a competitive skier, and a former lingerie model, that doesn't mean that you don't have a brain in that pretty little head of yours, does it? To prove this, you should occasionally remind her that it's not easy remembering which market gets the double order of sourdough and which favors the rye.

You should be aware of a speed bump that may occur in a relationship like this: her children. If they are not older than you, they are about your age. Even so, it is important that you present a paternal image to her son, even though

you will have absolutely no dad duties in respect to him. This image may be difficult to maintain, however, seeing that in college, he was a pledge in your fraternity when you were chairman of the "Throw Up or Throw Down" committee. Likewise, keep an arm's-length relationship with your new "daughter." Sure, she's hot and you've seen her at clubs, but leave it there. No massages, no hot tubs, no pillow fights, and no staying up half the night with her and her friends telling ghost stories.

As for your ten-year-old son, he will come to appreciate the amenities of your new lifestyle. When he comes to visit on weekends, not only will he have his own room, but he will also have his own guesthouse, horse, and manservant named Paco.

But remember that you are still his dad and role model. So you need to make sure that he gets to bed at a proper time, eats a balanced diet, and stays away from the top drawer of your dresser, where you keep the buttless chaps that you wear with pride whenever your wife tells you to.

TWENTY

FIRE UP THE BLENDER

There is a rising percentage of dads in this country and around the world who don't fit neatly into the concept of the nuclear family. Gone are the days where virtually every household was *Ozzie and Harriet* or *Father Knows Best*. Today we have blended families, single parent families, and everything in between. It's not uncommon for grandparents to be raising their grandchildren; for stay-at-home dads to juggle housework with homework, baseball with ballet; or for single parents to manage raising their kids while working increasing hours and still carving time for a social life. No longer are booster seats for children incompatible with "Early Bird Specials." Moms are at the park coaching soccer, while dads are at home burning the pot roast.

Same-sex dads struggle with raising children the same as no-sex dads.

But no matter what type of family tree you find yourself happily perched in, there's no denying one thing: you are the dad.

To your children, you are the one who provides the comic relief. You are the one who provides an environment so Mom can do her best work. You are the one who provides a shoulder to cry on and a wallet to ransack.

You are a bicycle-chain fixer, a soccer ball pumper-upper, a barbecuer, and an "I-think-you're-beautiful" affirmer.

You are a stay-up-till-2-AM worrier, a Saturday-morning-donut getter, a story-when-I'm-sick reader, an on-your-shoulders carrier, and a really goofy dancer.

You are a dad.

And someday, if the forces of nature sign off on it, you will know the happiness of being a daughter-down-the-aisle walker. Or a "we are so proud to have you for a daughter-in-law" toaster.

And then, the ultimate: a grandchild holder, spoiler, and pictures on the refrigerator hanger.

When some dads get reflective—which is usually after enjoying a few beers or sex—they often wonder if they've imparted enough important life lessons to their children. Things like "Buy low, sell high"; "Let your handshake be your promise"; and "Never be too proud to help someone who needs it."

That just goes to show you what alcohol and sex can do to your brain. Most dads never say that kind of stuff to their kids. We're more like: "Never drive behind a man with a hat on"; "Never hit a chip shot when you can putt instead"; and "Aluminum cans keep brews colder than glass." That's it; nothing earthshaking. Just little bits of stuff we've picked up. Hopefully, instead of *saying* what's important, we *live* it. And we do it without even knowing it.

But there are times, particularly when your children are between the ages of seventeen and twenty-four, when you will wonder if they even know you are there at all. When you start to consider this, you might ask yourself, "Is it really such a wonderful life?"

Relax. Give it time.

Because the day will come when they become dads themselves. You may be over at your son's house when he will yell at one of his kids, "Hey, you think I'm air conditioning the whole neighborhood? Close the door!"

You smile. Wonder where he got that?

Or when you call him on your seventieth birthday to tell him that you and his mother are going skydiving next week. There will be a pause, and then you will hear him pounding his phone on his kitchen table. Then he'll get back on the phone and say, "Sorry, Dad, my phone's not working right. What did you say again?"

That's your boy.

So if you've gotten to the grown kids, out of the house stage, it's time for you to sit back and reminisce about a job well done. Not only have you taught your kids some things, but you've also learned a lot yourself: kids really don't like sarcasm, unless they're delivering it; it's abundantly clear that they will treat their mom the same way you do; and trying to learn how to text after the age of forty-five may not be the best use of your time.

But you also missed a couple of lessons along the way. Like you never got around to teaching your son that trick we all learned in high school, where you hold a bottle cap between your thumb and middle finger and flick it so is floats across the room like a mini-Frisbee.

But hey, nobody's perfect, so all we can advise is that you enjoy the ride—every twist and turn and tire-squealing moment of it. There is nothing quite as satisfying and life-affirming as raising a baby to adulthood and realizing that there is now another very decent human being on the planet.

And this satisfaction shouldn't diminish one bit when the doorbell rings, and there stands your offspring, backpack slung over his shoulder, a suitcase on one hand and a guitar in the other, wondering if he can drop anchor at home until he can sort things out. Heck, that's what you're there for, right? And this'll finally give you time to teach him that whole bottle cap thing.

ACKNOWLEDGMENTS

MIKE:

I'd like to applaud my boys, John and Kevin Milligan, for their amazing humor and love over the course of my "Dad" career. You guys have always managed to keep it very interesting. And Jill, thanks and eternal devotion for putting up with bad backs and even worse moods. Love you all mucho.

Tombo? What can I say?

Mark Weinstein at Skyhorse: Thanks once more for the nice editing. What's next?

Dan Lazar at Writers House: Hooray!

Adam Wallenta: Great illustrations . . . again.

TOM:

To Tyler and Ian Lynch, who gave me the "Dad" qualifications to be a part of this book. To all the dads who have risen to the occasion, I offer my thanks and admiration. Those who have affected me and my outlook most include Toby, Brian, Mike, Norm, Frank, and Kevin. Keep up the good work guys—there's no more important job on earth.

ABOUT THE AUTHORS

Michael Milligan has been a television comedy writer and producer for over thirty years. Among his credits are *The Jeffersons, All In The Family, Dear John, Here and Now,* and *Fatherhood.* He is also the author of the books *Grandpa Rules*, and, with his wife, Jill, *Grandma Rules* and *Mom Rules.* Michael and Jill live in Southern California.

Tom Lynch has spent the last twenty years as a story analyst, identifying and developing screenplays for some of the biggest movie studios in Hollywood. Prior to that, he was a helicopter pilot, working around the world, from the steaming jungles of Vietnam and New Guinea to the sands of the Persian Gulf and the mountains of Alaska. Yet some of his most dangerous and exciting assignments took place at the wheel of the family van as an operational dad under the command of his wife, Cookie.

Mike and Tom have been goofing off together since high school.